THE
PHILANTHROPIST'S
TALE

THE
PHILANTHROPIST'S
TALE

The Life of Laurie Marsh

BY
LAURIE MARSH

urbanepublications.com

Published in Great Britain in 2016 by Urbane Publications Ltd
Suite 3, Brown Europe House, 33/34 Gleamingwood Drive, Chatham, Kent ME5 8RZ

A CIP catalogue record for this book is available from the British Library.

ISBN 9781910692547

Design and Typeset by Julie Martin
Cover design by The Invisible Man

Printed and bound by CPI Group (UK) Ltd, Croydon, CR0 4YY

urbanepublications.com

'A humanist in word and deed, Laurie's sustained generosity through his charitable efforts provides an inspiration for those who seek to make a difference from an entrepreneur's standpoint. What better crowning achievement to a lifetime of business success than to let the fruits of that success be shared with so many people less fortunate.'

Andrew Copson, Chief Executive,
British Humanist Association

'Dr Laurie Marsh is a true philanthropist. He has generously supported MSF for many years, showing extraordinary commitment to the organisation. He trusts us to spend the funding as we see fit, allowing us to provide medical aid to the people who need it most, no matter where they are or whether they have hit the headlines. Support from dedicated individuals like Dr Marsh means MSF can be completely independent and impartial, which is central to our values. We wish Dr Marsh every success with his book and look forward to reading his story!'

Hannah Richardson, Médecins Sans Frontières/
Doctors Without Borders (MSF UK)

'There are many successful entrepreneurs in the world, but few that genuinely share that success to help others. From clothing manufacturer to property magnate, movie producer to champion of charity, Laurie's tale will astonish, entertain, amaze and inspire as he ultimately reveals the true secret of success – that the only challenge we ever need is the next one.'

The Lord Rix of Whitehall

'Laurie Marsh is not just a successful entrepreneur. He epitomises how the many years of his business experience can be employed so effectively for philanthropic ends and the benefit of important causes.'

Simon Ross, Chief Executive, Population Matters

'Theatre, film gossip, insider stories – AND – a ground-breaking approach to supporting our essential services by sustaining our arts and culture – what's not to love? Laurie Marsh is an exciting and innovative economic thinker and doer – and what he does works!'

Martin Humphries, Director
The Cinema Museum, Elephant & Castle, Lambeth/
Southwark borders

For Gillian; Liz; my children Mandy, Robert & Katie; and my grandchildren Clemmie, Lizey and Frankie.

INTRODUCTION

I'd always known it was going to be an awkward evening. We've all had experiences like the one I was about to have. You know, when you are invited around for supper with a couple who are clearly not getting along. It never ends well. What made this slightly different was one half of the warring couple was an internationally recognisable actress from the much-loved TV show *The Avengers* and the other, a respected but relatively unknown artist.

At the time of the fateful dinner party it was already well-known in the arts community that the marriage between Avengers girl Diana Rigg and Israeli artist Menachem Gueffen was not entirely harmonious. In an interview Diana had talked about the relationship and even joked that "I give the marriage a year". There were persistent rumours that during their stay at his home in Israel, Menachem had kicked her out and then tossed her clothes through the window after her. I'd already had some first-hand experience of the volatility between the two after he had arranged an exhibition of his work at a gallery in Mount Street, Mayfair. Diana asked me to come to the preview and to bring a bunch of friends, which I did. I was left with a lasting impression that, while he might be a talented painter and she a magnificent actress, they were clearly not suited.

I had known Diana for a while, so when Diana asked

me around to the dinner at her home in in Castlenau, Barnes, I didn't hesitate. I was, however, more than a little apprehensive about what lay ahead. It didn't take long before my worst fears were realised. Our glasses were barely charged for the pre-dinner drinks before Menachem began to goad Diana. Even though we were only exchanging small talk, he managed to find fault with pretty much everything being said. Frankly, it was becoming exhausting finding non-controversial subjects. To make matters even more awkward, Menachem did not even join us at the table.

For a while, I did my best to let it all wash over me, but as the evening went on it became clear that Menachem thought I was having an affair with his wife. He was of course utterly wrong; having added two and two and made five. The writing was on the wall, the dinner did not end well and, hardly surprisingly, shortly afterwards Diana's marriage ended in divorce, after just three years as man and wife. Diana stayed in touch; after all, we had a good deal of respect for each other. I was privileged to have been able to spend quite some time with one of the most glamorous and sought after actresses of the time.

Intriguingly though, Diana was not the only Avenger I was close to. Indeed, I was linked with all *three* of the female leads in *The Avengers* and also the actress in the revival of the secret agent series, *The New Avengers*. I don't think there are many people that can claim to be so fortunate as to have spent time close to all four Avengers.

The first Avenger I really got to know was Linda

Thorson, who was in fact, the last in the line-up of three girls who played the lead in the original *The Avengers* series. She followed Diana Rigg, who played *Emma Peel,* who in turn followed Honor Blackman who played *Cathy Gale.* I met Linda, who played sporty *Tara King* in the Sixties cult show, when she came to see me at Tigon Films about a part we were casting. We got on well immediately. It wasn't just that she was very attractive, with an outgoing personality, but had a sharp wit and feisty attitude. We dated for a short time and then she moved in with me. She and I lived together on and off for the next three and a half years. I say on and off because Linda was getting quite a bit of TV and theatrical work at the time. On a couple of occasions, she would be out of London for a month or so after she accepted short provincial runs.

Enjoying an evening with Linda Thorson, and Graham and Audrey Stark

There were a couple of amazing incidents during our time together, which I shall not forget in a hurry. In May 1975, we were tucked up in bed in our mews house when the telephone on my side table rang. I took the call and found it an unfamiliar American voice on the other end.

'Is Curly Top there?' he drawled. 'Tell her it's the MAN.'

'Linda, it's an American asking for Curly Top,' I said, slightly non-plussed as I handed her the phone.

'Jesus!' She whispered. 'It's Frank!'

It was indeed non-other than the legendary crooner Frank Sinatra. Linda sounded bright and breezy as she spoke to her caller, but it was obvious it was an awkward situation, if only to me.

'Frank, I am here with my boyfriend Laurie and we are in bed. It is night-time here. It is not a good time to talk!'

There was some conversation from his end and he was clearly not bothered by her domestic situation. Clasping her hand over the receiver, she whispered to me: 'He wants me to go to the Cannes Film Festival with him'.

I gave her a look.

'Sorry Frank, no can do.'

Some hasty goodbye words were said and she gave the phone back to me with an apologetic what-can-you-do shrug.

The following year, we were travelling in the USA and we decided to visit Palm Springs around March time. Linda casually said: 'Maybe we can meet up with Frank. He has a gorgeous home there on Sinatra Drive.'

Frank had, by this time, married Barbara Marx. We did meet up with them and to my enormous surprise we were invited to Passover Dinner. Unbelievable!

Linda and I also visited Run Run Shaw in Hong Kong while we were together. Run Run was the amazing owner of Shaw Film Studios where the first King Fu films were made, but more of that later. He died at the astonishing age of 107, in January 2014.

The trip came about after we decided to fly to Hong Kong following a safari in Kenya. During our stay in Africa our hotel room was broken into and most of our clothes and possessions taken. Hardly surprisingly, we decided to leave Mombasa, and I called Run Run in Hong Kong. He was delighted that we were coming and agreed to have us met at the airport. What actually transpired was quite extraordinary. No sooner had we landed, there was an announcement over the plane's public address system that asked us to leave the plane first. Talk about star treatment. We walked down the steps to be greeted by a chauffeur with a long wheel-base limo. We did not even go through customs or set foot in the airport building. Run Run obviously had some serious influence. A separate vehicle brought our (virtually empty) bags to a suite in The Hyatt that he had arranged for us. The following evening, he arranged to have one of the lots at his film studios converted into a grand banqueting hall with chandeliers and a white-gloved member of staff serving each guest. We were the guests of honour, together with the High Commissioner and Police Chief, as well as some famous Chinese actors. The Chinese food and setting was amazing.

Linda had earlier introduced me to Diana Rigg,

although she subsequently regretted it. I was particularly busy running many projects at the time and somewhat blotted my copybook when I brought Diana home after an evening out and Linda was upstairs at 1 Albert Terrace Mews with a dreadful dose of flu. Nothing untoward happened, but Linda went berserk when I returned from taking Diana home. She flew at me in a complete rage.

'How dare you bring Diana here, when I am ill in bed,' she shrieked.

I was suitably chastened and in later years I understood why this behaviour had not gone down well; but right then, I was recently divorced and rather enjoyed the attention of all these beautiful women. You live and learn though!

My relationship with Honor was completely platonic. My very dear friend Brian Rix and his wife Elspet introduced us because they had been close friends for years. Honor proved to be just as charming and beautiful as her fellow Avengers and I have a lovely photo of us together at Brian and Elspet's 60th wedding anniversary party cruising down the Thames.

The final Avenger to cross my path was the lovely Joanna Lumley. We met towards the end of my own career in films. I had sold the majority of my interests to Lew Grade's company, Associated Communications Corporation, and while on the main board, I was trying to establish good relationships with my co-directors. Although I didn't know it then, my exit would be a lot faster than I had imagined, but more of that anon. Joanna was making a TV series for the company, so we'd met a few times. We must have got on fairly well, because she turned to me when she had a problem on set. It appeared the studio bosses were failing to close the large stage doors and she was constantly fighting colds thanks to the icy draught.

'I'm sure you've got a lot better things to be dealing with, but I really would appreciate your help with this,' she purred in that delightful voice of hers.

I immediately picked up the phone to the studio foreman and said something along the lines of: 'Close that door, or you'll walk out through it!'

The door problem was immediately dealt with and I received another call from Ms Lumley, who told me I was wonderful. We became good friends and went out on a number of subsequent occasions, such as film premieres and theatre first nights, and she was always very willing to help out when I needed a glamorous name to help on publicity.

As the stories here show, I've been tremendously fortunate in my career which spans more than 60-years. As well as these leading ladies, I have also met, and been close friends with, some of the best-known names in theatre, film and commerce, from entertainers such as Larry Hagman, Tom Conti, Richard Attenborough, Brian Rix and Ray Cooney, the Wiere Brothers and Boris Karloff, to businessmen at the top of their profession such as Harold Furst, Eric Reynolds, and Jack Rose.

In *The Philanthropist's Tale*, I've tried to tell the full and frank story of how I built up my businesses and became involved in the heady world of show business. Although the most well-known of my work has been, and still is, in stage and screen, I have also had a wide and varied career elsewhere. I built up one of the UK's largest property companies out of a handful of shops in South London, as well as running a hugely successful network of town markets. And, in recent years, I have been involved in a large number of philanthropic ventures.

I've tried to tell the stories about how it all happened as best as I am able to, keeping as close to the way things unfolded as I can. I've been honest about the mistakes I've made along the way, the things I've done well and the bits I probably shouldn't have done. I've had some fantastic adventures, met some extraordinary people and enjoyed the company of some supremely talented individuals.

It's always difficult to look back on a life and work out how the various pieces came together, particularly when I have had such a varied and fascinating career. One moment I would be negotiating with an 'A' list actor, and the next I'd be in boots and a hard hat working out the best site for a new office complex. If I had to single out one element that has made a difference to my approach in life, it is that I have always tried to think laterally and react quickly to a change of circumstances, however unexpected it may be. I know there is always a way around a problem, even if it is not immediately obvious. And it doesn't matter what you do, as long as you enjoy it.

But, don't let me give it all away now. The stories are all in here, so I will let you judge for yourself.

I hope that reading this book is almost as interesting, fun and exciting as it was for me living through the events I describe, and that it captures at least some of the spirit and pleasure I felt during my career. No matter what I achieved, I've never lost sight of the fact that I was born into relative poverty, living over a Katz family haberdashery shop at 175 Lambeth Walk ... it's been a wonderful journey!

CHAPTER ONE

Showbiz types often talk about the entertainment business being in their blood. It is as though they couldn't avoid the inexorable draw of the stage or screen. Was that the case for me? I didn't think so, but try as I might, I never seemed to stray too far from the footlights.

My father provided my first brush with theatre. He had a great temperament and was a jack-of-all-trades; a skilled carpenter, electrician and builder. In fact, he could turn his hand to just about any practical task and invariably did. From a very young age I was aware that there was one activity that excited and satisfied him above all others: performing. In his spare time, he was Dave Evad (eagle-eyed readers will note the surname is simply the first name in reverse). He would leave our home in Lambeth and head to venues throughout London to entrance and amaze his audience with his magic tricks.

In later years I was curious about why he loved the stage so much. He was never what you might call a sociable person. In fact, he far preferred the company of animals to humans. When he wasn't on stage or working, he would regularly go off horse riding in the countryside outside London; and when he was at home, dogs and horses seemed to seek out his company.

Thinking back to the few times I saw him on stage, I suspect he warmed to it because, as a performer, he was slightly removed from his audience. They would gaze at him in rapt attention, lapping up his tricks and illusions, many of which he actually constructed himself with a little help from me. When I went on stage with him at the Regal Kennington, aged no more than 8-years old, I could hardly imagine how he could do such a thing. I was only acting as an assistant, mutely handing him props, but I was acutely aware that behind the glare of the lights hundreds of people were watching us.

The Regal Kennington was an exciting venue. Albert O'Connor, who had made his money with a chain of West End milk bars called Black and White, decided to sell them and to invest the proceeds into building The Regal in 1932. This was an era when music hall was still popular country-wide, but cinema was threatening to capture an ever-growing share of the entertainment market. No one really knew whether moving pictures would replace music halls. Mr O'Connor decided to hedge his bets and built a giant auditorium which could double up as both a cinema *and* a music hall.

Dad introduced me to Mr O'Connor. He was slim, rather good-looking man and always wore a three-piece formal suit. Whenever there was a U-certificate film showing, I would walk boldly past the doorman (with his peaked cap, shiny buttons and polished shoes) and up the wide staircase to the boss' office.

'Mr O'Connor, I would like to see this film,' I'd announce.

His face would always crinkle into a smile and he'd rummage in his desk drawer to find me a complimentary ticket. I'd thank him and walk back downstairs and present the ticket to the uniformed attendant. In those days, it was quite usual to have 20 or more uniformed staff. As far as I knew, I was the only person who ever got a complimentary ticket, and it began my love affair with cinema – a love that has lasted throughout my life. Funnily enough, as a BAFTA voting member and Cinema Veteran I still don't pay for cinema tickets today!

My trips to the Regal Kennington were a highlight in an otherwise unremarkable early childhood. My parents rented three shops. One was a general store which sold everything from razor blades to perfume, tobacco and snuff. 180 Lambeth Walk, next to our shop at 178, was leased by the Fromberg family who sold wool, cotton and knitting patterns. When they moved out in 1936, we agreed to take over their lease and sold greeting cards and stationery. The third shop was a hairdressing salon called Dorella, which my mum ran on a part-time basis, managing along the way to launch the careers of many well-known West End coiffeurs such as Teasy Weasy.

My parent's marriage certificate shows my dad listing himself as a master tobacconist. He and his father had a thriving business importing tobacco from what was then Rhodesia and Virginia, and he would blend it on a big black pan on the kitchen stove. The resulting concoction was then packaged and sold for pipe smokers, or made into cigarettes at the famous Black Cat factory, that also made Craven A cigarettes for Imperial Tobacco. My father and grandfather were very successful importers of Swedish matches too, until competitors did what they always do and began to capture more and more and more of the market by cutting prices. The profits from matches and clay pipes, which my family also imported, dropped significantly. One company after the other went out of business. In the end, the very large wooden cases the packages of matches were delivered in from Sweden were actually worth more than the product inside. My father and grandfather saw the writing on the wall and got out of the business, which was a shame because they were close to making it big before the price war. Loose tobacco remained a big seller in the poorer parts of London.

Ever the entrepreneur, my old man pretty soon began to announce himself as a 'manufacturing chemist' because he had begun buying in products on a bulk-buy, wholesale basis and then divide them up into smaller units. I would join in with his new business, bottling liquids such as olive oil, washing up liquid and paraffin – the job I hated most was sticking the labels on each of the bottles. Still, it worked out well for dad. Years later, when he was called-up into the army towards the end of the Second World War, he was put into the Royal Army Medical Core on the strength of his calling card as a 'manufacturing chemist'.

When I was born in number 175, on 23 October 1930, I was the third generation of my family to live on Lambeth Walk. My mother's parents lived and worked in 'The Walk', as we knew it, after immigrating to the UK in 1896 from Russia. My grandmother Leah, whose family name was Katz, held on to her immigration papers which bore her thumb print, rather than a signature.

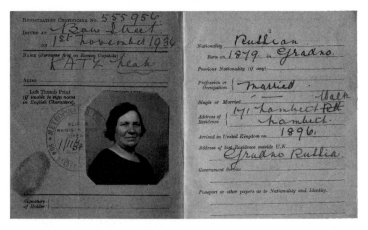

My grandmother's Naturalization Document

She gave birth to my mother and five other children at 171 Lambeth Walk. We were part of a close-knit family community. Indeed, mother's three sisters Bertha, Mabel and Queenie, and her two brothers, Izzy and Joe, lived above the shoe shop at 171 Lambeth Walk. My father, who was born opposite at number 162, worked with his father and brother, who was yet another Izzy (it was a popular name for that generation of Jewish boys), in their tobacconist shop. Izzy's two children, Leslie & Monty, lived there too. They have always been really close to me, and they are still even though geography now separates us. They moved from The Walk to Stamford Hill, and then on to Cardiff at the beginning of the war.

My maternal grandparents owned two shops, a shoe shop and a haberdashery, which were separated by a butcher's. We lived over the haberdashers. Our home was a simple two room flat which had no toilet, electricity or heating. We were never struggling, but we were never what anyone would call comfortably off either. Our already uncomfortable situation was made all the more cramped because we were obliged to keep Zoa, an enormous German Shepherd dog, to hold the rats at bay. Rodents thrived in the yard behind the butcher's shop. On the plus side, Zoa doubled up as a very capable nanny for me when I was left on my own, and if anyone came closer than he thought was necessary, he would bare his teeth and growl. On reflection, this may have been why I didn't have too many friends when I was small! I don't remember this, but my mother told me that she used to leave me with Zoa in the sandpit by the Thames for a few hours, while she was busy running her two shops. It was only a few hundred yards away, but it certainly wouldn't be acceptable today.

Not the famous Zoa, but another canine friend from my youth!

While my family was at the centre of a close-knit community, surrounded by various uncles, aunts and cousins who took up most of The Walk, I didn't have what might be called a 'secure' childhood. I was aware from a very early age that my parents didn't particularly have lot of time for me. Having children was simply what you did in those days. The fact I remained an only child was testament to how little my mum and dad enjoyed the experience the first time around. To be fair to my mother, she didn't have a very good time giving birth to me and she had already been through the trauma of losing a premature boy who only survived for a few weeks after he was born. That experience understandably gave her pause. It probably didn't help that I also decided to put in an appearance early. I was nearly two months premature. In the ensuing panic, the local quack, Dr McLoughlin, had to deliver me using forceps. Having met him on a few subsequent occasions during my childhood, when it was very evident he had been on the Irish whiskey, I have no doubt he was well lubricated throughout the inevitable trauma of my delivery. Indeed, a bottle of the hard stuff was apparently the payment he demanded for his toils. Either way, he certainly seemed to have a fairly relaxed attitude to my survival. I was plonked unceremoniously into a cotton-wool lined boot-box, no doubt donated by Uncle Joe and his wife Gertie from my grandparents' shoe shop.

There was serious doubt that I would make it. Paddy McLoughlin kept an eye on me and against the odds, I survived. My birth was not registered until 30th December.

Although my mother clearly did what needed to be done, I was always left with a sense she had too much to do in the shops to really spend much time with me. We became closer once I started to help out in the shop. This was as soon as I could see over the counter, and I quickly learned how to give change.

My father was not around for much of the time. I realised in later life that, as well as the conjuring, horse-riding and his range of business activities, his attention was easily taken by a pretty face. He had a number of girlfriends over the years. I found out, quite recently, that he had even fathered another child – so I had a half-brother. It was a scandal the family kept to themselves though. It all happened before my parents were married. The baby's mother was not Jewish, which made the event even more appalling to my deeply religious paternal grandparents, and they briefly threw my father out of the house. They patched things up eventually and clearly decided the best way to deal with the 'mistake' was never to speak of it.

It didn't cure my father of his wandering eye, though he always came home eventually. Mum also had the odd dalliance, I believe. She was certainly quite close to a fireman who worked out of the London Fire Brigade's HQ on the Thames Embankment. I suspect this liaison might have been more about revenge on my dad, rather than a burning passion (no pun intended), but I never asked. At least she was always there for me, in body if not in mind. She had a lot going on, making ends meet.

King George V's death in January 1936 marked the

beginning of a terrible year. There was a real feeling of sadness around the Walk and it was compounded by the death of my mum's mother Leah, in the same year. Her husband Victor, who had developed Parkinson's Disease early on in his life, was heartbroken. Eventually, he was shipped off to Blackpool to a care home to avoid the blitz in London, and was never told that his youngest offspring, Izzy, had been killed – although this was not totally unusual amongst families at that time. I can still remember travelling to Blackpool by train a few times with my mother. It took all day and when we got there I would be rewarded with all sorts of unbelievable stories from grandpa about the Tsar's Cossack soldiers riding through his shtetl and chopping up any Jews they could catch.

With all this going on around me I felt I had to become completely self-sufficient, keeping my emotions to myself. Inevitably I grew into a quiet, studious child who was a little withdrawn. A bout of measles left me with poor eyesight. My parents didn't know that they were supposed to keep me in a darkened room when the disease was at its height, in order to protect my eyes. As a result, my left eye was particularly badly affected. No other kid on the street wore glasses and those kids around me wasted no time in calling me goggle-eye Jew-boy.

When I was five, my mother told me that I was going to school to 'learn in a class'. I thought she said 'learn at a glass' and was quite intrigued when I was taken for my first day at Lollard Street Mixed Infants School, the nearby Primary. I was really surprised that there was no glass involved, and even more so that I was expected to go

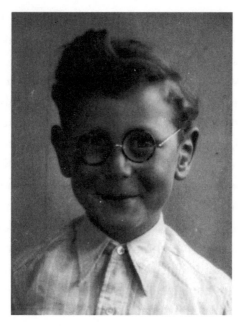

The 'goggle-eye Jew-boy'

back the following day. My mother and I had quite a row about that.

The local Lambeth youth were pretty unwelcoming to someone like me. Not only did I look geeky and bookish, thanks to my specs, but the fact that I was Jewish really made me stand out. London in the pre-war years was no different from much of the rest of Europe, and anti-Semitic behaviour was noticeably on the rise. While there were many communities who were strongly supportive of British Jews, there were many who were not and they weren't afraid to make their feelings known.

From the moment I joined Lollard Street I was singled out. There was no question of segregating religions in those days, so it was very obvious that I wasn't joining in the compulsory morning prayers. On good days, if I was very lucky, it just led to name-calling and taunting.

'You killed Jesus,' they'd chant, as though I had personally been responsible for the crucifixion.

Some days though, the abuse escalated to became physical. Boys would deliberately shove me aside in the corridor, or 'accidently' barge into me in the small outside play-ground, their bony elbows jabbing sharply into my ribs. If that didn't get a good enough reaction, a couple would gang up, their fists flaying, showering me with as many insults as they could think up between blows. I quickly became a very fast runner, rather like Tom Hanks playing Forrest Gump. At the first sign of trouble, I would hare off down the street like an Olympic sprinter. I wasn't always quick enough though. Sometimes I didn't see it coming and I would be trapped, cornered like some desperate animal, terrified by the inevitability of what I knew was about to happen.

The violence wasn't sophisticated. The blow I dreaded most was one to my face. Invariably, a head shot led to my glasses flying off and breaking. Yet again I would be back to see Mr Jackson and would have to witness his oh-so-patient shake of the head and barely audible tut. Mr Jackson kept a jeweller's half-shop, five doors down from my parent's. He invariably had at least one pair of my glasses in for repair. I would swap the mangled pair for the mended ones and escape as quickly as I could.

It was obvious the situation couldn't continue indefinitely, so I decided to fight back: literally. There was a local tailor called Joe Emdon; his shop was ranged over two floors and he'd cut fabrics on a large table on the first floor and drink tea with customers on the ground floor. I wasn't interested in his suit-making or his refreshments though. Joe was a professional boxer before he became a tailor and when he offered to give me a few pointers I leapt at the chance.

'I'll teach you how to protect yourself,' he promised, after seeing my bruised face and taking pity on me. 'It's all about using your arms properly to stop the blows landing.'

•••

The Second World War, which began when I was nine, meant very little to me to start with. I had heard adults talking about the prospect of another 'Great War' for so long that when it was finally declared it felt like it had been going on for years already. I was a little curious about the prospect of the blanket bombing raids everyone had been talking about.

'London is going to be reduced to smouldering rubble,' grown-ups would say darkly, peering up at the sky, as though they expected to see a German bomber sweeping low at any moment.

When the bombs did eventually start raining down, it was terrifying. My dad and my mother's brother Izzy joined the ARP and spent some nights collecting incendiary bombs that had failed to explode. I hid in a cupboard under the stairs, but the whole house would shake. Each bomb that went off created such a noise I thought my eardrums would explode too. I couldn't get a wink of sleep and dreaded the time when dusk crept up at the close of the day. It wasn't long before there was talk of evacuation.

'Laurie has to go to a Jewish place,' my mother would insist.

Right then though, there were very few places opening their doors to Jews. Schools had been given their dreaded quotas for Jewish children, and many were already stuffed full with the children who had escaped from mainland Europe.

The final straw that concentrated their minds was when Uncle Izzy was killed in early 1941 during a particularly severe bombing raid. He was a kind, handsome, gentle man who ran the haberdashery shop over which I was born. The shop was handed over to Auntie Queenie.

'You are going to Brighton,' announced my father a short while later.

'Brighton?' I said, surprised and not a little concerned. 'That's on the coast. Isn't that exactly where the Germans are going to try and invade?'

'There is a Jewish prep school there and they intend to evacuate to the countryside in South Gloucestershire where you will be safe.'

I was distraught. My parents wanted me to be safe but they had provided the only home I ever knew. Besides, I had never been to the countryside before. I had no idea what to expect. How would I cope? And South Gloucestershire? It might have well been on the South Pole for all I knew about it. It felt awfully far away from London; for the first time in my life I felt truly alone.

After a few weeks in Brighton, a teacher arranged for

us all get into a coach and we got off at Cromhall, near the village of Charfield, in South Gloucestershire.

'Follow me,' said, a balding, tall and well-dressed man. This was Mr Lyon-Maris, the Headmaster of Beaconsfield College in Cromhall. I hoped his curtness was just the result of an off day, or perhaps he was a little overwhelmed by the number of evacuees descending on the area. I was not in luck. Mr Lyon-Maris was a sadistic, unpleasant man. He had received his degree in teaching in Canada and it wasn't long before we were all saying, 'He should not be allowed to teach us in England'. All sense of relief that I had escaped my schoolboy tormentors in Lollard Street was replaced by a permanent sense of fear about what dreadful punishment the Headmaster would inflict next. What made it all the more terrifying was there was no sense of consistency to the man. He was utterly unpredictable. To make matters worse, he ran his school by a ridiculous set of rules. The children were all sent to bed at 6 o'clock, even though bright sunlight flooded through our flimsy curtains until gone 10pm in the summer. Any boys who dared to whisper, let alone talk, were dragged from their bed and beaten with a cane until they bled. Mr Lyon-Maris seemed to have no moral compass whatsoever.

There were a few light moments, thanks to the other children, who were in the same boat as me. I fell completely in love with a Kinder refugee from Germany, called Ilsa Meryn, but never summoned up the courage to express my feelings. I also made a number of friends. The Beaconsfield College theatre also provided some much-needed levity. I enjoyed performing, although my acute shyness with girls did earn me the odd clip around the ear. In one play, I was a prince but because I baulked at kissing my co-star Barbara's hand in one scene, Mr Lyon-Maris gave me a firm whack around the head. Most of the time I simply lived from one day to the next, just doing my best to survive the experience.

My already low opinion of the Headmaster plummeted even further when I saw him smash a gramophone record into pieces one day. Mr Lyon-Maris had always made a great deal of fuss about his music collection and regularly travelled to Bristol to pick up new recordings. He would then set up his gramophone player at the head of the class and we would listen to the record in dutiful silence. I didn't mind that. It was one of the few things that seemed to make him happy, which meant we weren't in immediate danger and I always loved listening to music. Then, one day, he put on a disc of *Oh! Danny Boy*, and settled into his chair. As always, his whole demeanour signalled that complete silence was required. Yet, we'd only been listening to the song for a minute or so when, inexplicably, Mr Lyon-Maris swept the disc off the gramophone player with a theatrical shake of his head.

'Utter rubbish,' he said to no one in particular.

To my horror, he gripped the disc in both hands and brought it sharply down across his knee, shattering it into jagged pieces. Still muttering he stalked out of the room, slamming the door behind him.

I was shaken to the core. My Auntie Mabel sold gramophone records and I wanted to save up to buy one. This wilful destruction of a disc was almost sacrilegious to my young mind. What sort of person would do something like that?

Not long after this incident, my cousin Geoffrey Cole, who lived in Cardiff, was sent to join me at Cromhall. He hated it. On the second day, he went into the garden shed toilet, locked and bolted the door and refused to come out. He stayed there for a whole day and that night his mother and father came to collect him. I gave some thought to emulating the exercise but dismissed it. I doubted the outcome would have been the same.

•••

It was a relief when I turned 11 and had to move on. At the time I didn't think I had benefited from the experience at all. Looking back now, I suppose the one thing I could say is it did actually provide me with a seriously good education. We were all too scared to avoid learning our lessons. However, after two years at the hands of Mr Lyon-Maris and his team, I left the school with the firm opinion there could be no worse school on the planet. I found out much later that a dear friend that I have known for 60 years, Marion Style, was evacuated to Beaconsfield College just after I left.

Once I returned to London, it was clear my parents still hadn't made any firm decisions on my future schooling options.

'There is something your grandpa Philip suggested, but it is quite a long shot,' my dad said. 'It's a school in Cambridge.'

My grandparents Philip and Rebecca (or Betty as everyone knew her), lived in Darenth Road, Stamford Hill in North London. It was an area with a high proportion of Jews. Jews had long been barred from a huge number of places, from hotels to football clubs, and there was a strict quota on the number of Jewish kids allowed to study in each public school. A number of additional measures were introduced both before and during World War Two, mainly to curb the rising numbers coming in from mainland Europe to escape Nazi brutality. Many of the bans didn't seem to make sense and the most recent ones clearly appeared to be politically motivated.

My grandfather Philip had done quite well for himself, building up a portfolio of half a dozen properties. A deeply religious man, he wanted to help the many others in the area that were less well off. His houses were all leased out for around £1 a week and, as we later discovered, the maintenance costs and overheads were higher than the income. So, while grandpa was converting the income from his tobacco shops into properties, his motivation was not particularly commercially orientated. However, he was extremely well-regarded in the community.

'Grandpa has been speaking to Dr Jay, who lives on the corner of Darenth Road,' my dad continued. 'He has two sons, Barry and Ian, and they've both got a place at this very famous old school. Apparently, it doesn't have a Jewish Quota. The doctor says you should try for a place too. The boys are both at boarding house called Hillel House. You'd have to sit a tough entrance exam and we'd have to pay fees for the boarding, but it's worth a try. There is a chance you could get a scholarship and that would really help.'

I didn't need any encouragement. If there was a hint of a chance of a decent school that was nothing like Beaconsfield College, I would have sat 100 scholarship exams.

Within days I was off to Cambridge on a train from Kings Cross and then onwards by the number 106 bus to the school, where I was to sit my exams. It wasn't half as daunting as being sent away from home the first time. I suppose the odious Mr Lyon-Maris had at least ensured I was reasonably well-educated self-reliant, even though I was just 11 years-old.

My first impressions of Hillel House and Perse School were that it was all quite intimidating. The school was opposite the city's cathedral and consisted of a large central hall with a number of full-length picture windows. It looked smart and well cared for, the polar opposite of Lollard Street and Cromhall.

After I sat the test I was taken on a tour of Hillel House, which had five dormitories on the first and second floors. One, which was for the youngest boys, was called Bantams, and Midgets was for boys between 8 and 10 years-old. I fell into the age category that occupied Rooms, which were for boys between 11 and 12 years-old and these had four beds. Then there was Little Dorm for boys up to the age of 15, and finally Big Dorm for the oldest boys. Downstairs, on the ground floor, was a Prep Room, where the prefects supervised us whilst we did our copious homework. There was also a library for the seniors, a washroom and a dining hall.

Harry Dagut, the Housemaster who showed me

around, explained the life of a junior was based on a strict routine. I would not be allowed out of the school to go into town (although we were all expected to walk the two miles to synagogue each Saturday), while Sunday afternoons were devoted to compulsory games. I didn't mind that. I loved sport and had become quite athletic ever since I had learned that running fast was the best way to evade bullies.

I had yet to show any serious academic prowess, but even at 11 years of age I could not help but be inspired by the glowing terms in which everyone at Perse School described the former Head Teacher Dr Rouse. Although Perse School was about 350 years-old, having been founded in 1615 thanks to a generous £10,000 legacy from a property developer called Stephen Perse, it had long been in decline until 1902 when Dr Rouse took-up his post. He was deemed to be quite the eccentric and had introduced a number of hugely successful experimental teaching methods, most notably the Direct Method of teaching foreign languages. Teachers who spoke each language were brought in and would only use the tongue in each lesson. Thus in a French lesson, all you would hear was French, in German lessons German and so on. It proved hugely effective. Not only had exam results improved dramatically, but news of this success attracted scores of talented teachers to the school. Before he retired in 1928, Rouse built a remarkable team of staff and the school had earned an international reputation. Rouse had also approved the formation of Hillel House, a Jewish boarding house without a quota, and was extremely keen to open up the school by offering as many free places to able students as possible, regardless of their ethnicity.

Even as I sat down, pen in hand, to take the entrance exam, I knew I had to pass. There was something about that school that immediately inspired my young self. The walls themselves seemed to ooze with encouragement and possibilities. There was a real buzz about the place. I felt I could achieve anything if I went there.

After an agonising wait, I got the news I had been praying for. I was in. I had passed with flying colours and was offered a scholarship too. However, while my schooling would be free, my parents would have to find the money for the boarding house fees. All credit to them, they agreed straight away. Even though they would have to scrimp and save, they could see this was an opportunity of a lifetime.

Despite being a little apprehensive and already a little homesick by the time I arrived in Cambridge, Harry Dagut and his wife, daughter and son were a wonderful family who quickly made us all feel at home.

I was keen on Art, English literature, French and sport. The latter three were under the guidance of Mr Keith Barry, who ran South Lodge with his wife Beryl (who had moved to Cambridge in 1935 from her native New Zealand). Keith was in his late twenties, slim and obviously athletic. He had a pleasant, gentle manner and while he was not afraid to enforce discipline as required, he generally relied on his tried and tested method of keeping order. He would take the opening class of the year and wait for the first boy to misbehave before getting him stand up in front of the rest of the class. A severe dressing down would ensue, followed by a punishing obligation to write a lengthy story. Keith Barry always said he had no trouble with the boys after that and he was right. It also helped that he had a light-hearted, easy-going attitude, which meant the boys instantly warmed to him. He was immensely proud of his new Triumph Roadster and could occasionally be persuaded to let up to four boys pile in for a spin. There would be two in the front, two more standing behind the front seat.

It was largely down to this Master and the other members of a great team that bullying was kept to a minimum at Perse. It was certainly nothing like Lollard Street when it came to discipline. The staff quickly dealt with any problems there were. The prefects also exercised excellent discipline.

I got on very well with most of the boys even though we all had quite different interests. Peter Hall, for example, who would one day become Sir Peter Hall, founder of the Royal Shakespeare Company, was already showing signs of a deeply held passion for drama. We became good friends in the early days, although Peter was always a little frustrated by my unwillingness to appear in his many shows. I just didn't like being one actor among many. Thanks to my dad, I was a boy who liked having the stage to myself. I didn't want to share it with dozens of other lads.

Then, there was Wally Olins, who would go on to become a national marketing guru and the architect of New Labour's 'Cool Britannia' image. He was already showing promise in English. While I was not at the top of any of the classes, I was invariably in the top three. My 'thing' was, as ever, magic. I used the conjuring tricks I had learned at my father's knee to gain certain kudos among my peers and the boys never seemed to tire of asking me to show them one trick after the other. Eventually, worn down by the constant chants of *'how did you do that?'* I agreed to start a magic club. It would, I warned, be an invitation only affair. The one unbreakable rule-of-entry was that no one would ever reveal to any outsiders the secrets I shared. That was non-negotiable. I even drew up a document to this effect, which everyone was required to sign with due solemnity.

My top secret conjuring notebook

The inevitable happened. One of the boys betrayed my trust and I knew, even at that young age, the disgust at this person's duplicitous behaviour would stay with me

H. H. M. C. To be kept.

I promise as a member of the H.H.M.C. That I keep the secrets of every ot illusion shown by the members.

To practise tricks and obey orders of the Pres., during meetings and practises.

To back up and uphold the club in every respect, and to KEEP ORDER during MEETINGS.

Having signed the promise you will be taken into full confidence of the club in every respect.

You are allowed to voice your opinion on any matter conected with the club.

Subscriptions will be very rare and obly taken with the consent of all. Donations by Hon members will be equally distributed For Buying Tricks ONLY.

SIGNED.   Date. Fri 28th May '46

N.B. Misbehaviour or Complete disregard to the club may result in Drastic Steps.

Lionel Lister...

S.W. Greenhill.

Dy. Fine. Sec.
L. Marsh. Pres

The strict rules of the H.H.M.C.

my whole life. The boy, Stanley Price (who later went on to become a renowned author), had signed my agreement, but the second he left the club he had bragged to anyone who would listen that he knew how the tricks worked. I was so furious that I challenged him to meet me in the Hillel House wooden scout hut (I have a lovely pencil drawing I did of this hut which was sadly pulled down quite recently). I intended to sort the matter out in time-honoured fashion. We both donned our boxing gloves and went at it, hammer and tongs. I'd obviously learned a thing or two from Joe Emden because I quickly subdued my opponent. We didn't speak again much after that day.

Competing in the long jump at the famous Fenner's Sports field, very close to the old Perse school

Despite the odd set back, such as the fight with Stanley, I could never lose sight of how much Perse School did for me. The school opened my eyes to a whole new world, a million miles beyond the yobbish behaviour I had been exposed to in my earlier childhood around Lambeth Walk and at Lollard Street. As I prepared to leave school after six and a half of the happiest years of my life, I had no real ideas yet about what I wanted to do for a career. I had qualified for the Higher School Certificate with distinction, but I could not get a place at that time at university, because they were all reserved for ex-military. I had no grand plans, I didn't quite know what the future held for me. I was, however, certain that I would mark my years at Perse School in some special way. I wanted to demonstrate my real gratitude.

Keith and I had grown quite close over the years and now I was on the cusp of adulthood I trusted him as an advisor, mentor and friend. Indeed, he had become like a second father to me. In more recent years, Keith had also taken on the task of raising funds for the school in addition to as well his role as a teacher and House Master.

As I travelled back to London, for the last time as a Perse School pupil, I already knew I'd never forget what that school had done for me. It hadn't just given me a top-notch education; it had given me confidence and poise. I'd learned that anything was possible with hard work and application. All I had to do now was to work out what it was I wanted to do and set my mind to it.

CHAPTER TWO

My attempts to sort out my hitherto un-structured grand plans had a number of false starts before they began to take any sort of shape. The first (and complete) non-starter was a putative career in dentistry. There had been an historic association with the profession in my family and my mother was very keen for me to uphold the tradition.

Back in the days when dentists practiced without any real qualifications, my grandmother Betty performed the service for the local community. People used to go to her and she'd pull their teeth if they had a problem. If any more than one or two teeth were playing up, she'd remove the whole lot and tell the poor patient to come back in a few weeks, whereupon she would give them some false teeth. Young people would have to come back again and again, to get successive sizes of teeth as they grew. When she died, we found boxes and boxes of false teeth in her bureau drawer.

For some reason, she wasn't the one to look after my ivories. That fell to a gentleman across the road called Mr Bloom. I still vividly remember the day my older cousin Monty had something wrong with one of his milk teeth and went across the road to consult Mr Bloom. The 'dentist' obligingly pulled out the offending tooth and I was flabbergasted when Monty told me his mum Rosie had given him a six pence piece for it when he took it home.

'Six pence?' I shrieked disbelievingly. 'That's a fortune! You could get three bars of Cadbury's chocolate with that.'

I was so upset by the perceived unfairness of it all, I immediately dashed across to Bloom and demanded that he pulled out one of my milk teeth too. He took out a loose tooth, gave it to me and I went home. I marched straight up to see my dad.

'Six pence please,' I said, holding my hand out to him with the bloody tooth placed strategically in the centre of my palm.

For a moment or two he looked confused, but then he chuckled and dug his hand into his trouser pocket. 'Here you go,' he said, still shaking his head and laughing to himself.

In between then and the time when I left Perse School, dentistry had become a bit more sophisticated. Patients certainly now expected anyone who worked on their teeth to have a professional qualification. My cousin, Leonard Wilder, was now a successful dentist and even broadcast on the radio about the subject. Another cousin, Monty (the one who'd got sixpence for the tooth all those years before), was also studying at Guys Hospital, although he was struggling to pass his exams.

'You could pass those exams easily and become a dentist,' announced my mother purposefully. 'Your grades in sciences are top notch and they certainly are good enough.'

She was right. I had passed the requisite chemistry, physics and Latin exams in my matriculation; the problem was I wasn't the least bit interested in becoming a dentist.

She didn't listen though and promptly arranged for me to meet some tutors at Guys Hospital.

'Do you think I should do it?' I asked Keith Barry, when we met up on one of his regular trips to London. The Perse Master was on countless committees, including the Oxford and Cambridge exam boards and we always met up when he was in town.

'Not if it doesn't interest you,' he said. 'It might be worth going along to hear what they have to say though.'

I attended the Guys meeting, but was saved from a real grilling from my parents by circumstance. A letter arrived to inform me that it was time to join the army. National Service was still compulsory then, even though the war was now over and it was painfully obvious my country had little need for the thousands of young men who were still being conscripted.

The letter said I needed to travel to Russell Square for a medical examination. I did so and was immediately pronounced 100 percent, A1, fit. It was hardly surprising really. I was not long out of Perse where we followed a rigorous physical routine. A few days later, I received a further communication confirming I had passed the medical and putting me on stand-by. It said I would receive the relevant documents and travel permits when they were ready for me.

It was a strange situation. The call-up basically said I had to be ready to go, but gave no indication of what date I might eventually be required. As I awaited my orders, I felt like I was in a strange kind of limbo. I obviously couldn't start anything significant, even though I was itching to get on with my life.

I was living in Conifer Gardens in Streatham with my parents, who had moved there while I was away at Perse. It felt strange going back there instead of to the Walk, but all of my father and mother's business interests were still in Lambeth, so I didn't leave the area of my childhood behind altogether. It was hard to know where I belonged and I ended up drifting for almost the entire year. I tried to keep myself busy by helping my father with his wholesale business, working in his shop and generally pottering around. It was singularly one of the most frustrating times of my life.

Eventually, to my relief, my call-up instructions arrived. I was to report to Catterick Camp in Yorkshire for training. My eagerness when I received this news wasn't down to the fact that I yearned for a career in the forces. I just wanted to get it over with so I could get on with the rest of my life.

My optimistic mood rapidly changed when I reached the camp. In fact, I don't know how they had the chutzpah to call it a 'camp'. My childhood home hadn't exactly been luxurious, but this was downright squalid. It was made up of a series of ramshackle huts, with wooden walls and broken windows. At the centre of each hut, which housed around a dozen conscripts, there was a large iron stove that provided the only form of heat. There was no source of hot water, so we used the tea from the canteen for washing and shaving. It came as no surprise to learn that these huts were condemned as uninhabitable in 1918.

'It's like a prison,' I said to the young lad who was standing beside me, after we were shown our home for the next six weeks.

'Right, you horrible lot,' roared an enrolment sergeant who was now looking around at us with a sneer.

I could hardly believe it. *Was he serious?* I'd never known anything like it. He was like a parody of an army sergeant shouting and stamping his feet, glaring at anyone that did anything out of turn.

As it turned out, he was serious. In fact, this man spent the next six weeks trying to break our spirits by shouting, bullying and generally demeaning us as much as he could. I could only suppose he had chosen this tactic to keep us occupied and maintain order because he recognised the real flaw in this entire charade – there was absolutely nothing for us to do.

My long-held misgivings about the pointlessness of National Service post the end of the Second World War were proved to be utterly correct. The entire period of training was spent cutting grass and painting buildings white. There was so little to do we even painted the coal, and cut the grass with clasp knives, literally one blade at a time. It was completely demoralising. Little wonder there was a popular saying – if it didn't move you painted it and if it did, you saluted it.

From my point of view, it was a total shock to the system. The life of a conscript was a million miles away from the ordered, stimulating and purposeful atmosphere of Perse. I couldn't stand wasting my time like this. Looking around at my fellow conscripts I was amazed that they seemed to be totally accepting of their lot. When I chatted to them in our hut, the over-riding attitude was: we're being paid for this, so what? They were clearly content to sit out their two years doing as little as possible, yet I had the feeling I might go out of my mind if I hung around that long.

I did everything I could to occupy myself and keep my brain functioning. I found out early on that I was the only man in the hut who could read and write to any degree. Most of the men could just about write their names and a few words with some difficulty, but when it came to composing letters home, forget it. These were, of course, the days before telephones were widely available, so the only way to communicate with loved ones was by mail. I quickly took on the role of chief letter writer and spent most evenings penning long affectionate letters to mums, dads and sweethearts I had never met and was never likely to do so either. My literary endeavours earned me the nickname Professor Marsh, which I rather liked. Despite doing my best to immerse myself in army life though, none of this was enough to keep me anywhere near fully stimulated. The days dragged by so slowly I thought they'd never end.

I decided on a self-preservation strategy of signing-up for every course going and as a result I was sent on a number of interesting jaunts which eventually led towards the Intelligence Corps. The fact I could speak four languages – English, French, German and Latin – was deemed a huge asset and I was promptly transferred to Maresfield in Sussex for further training. I kept thinking; *this is all very interesting, but it is not what I want to do*. I kept my thoughts to myself though, because anything was better than hanging around a broken-down hut in Catterick.

After my training at Maresfield I applied to the War Office Selection Board (WOSB) for officer training. Qualifying for a place meant being interrogated by a board of three officers to see if I had the 'right stuff'. I very quickly determined that the 'right stuff' meant good connections and the fact I had been to Perse public school was, rightly or wrongly, exactly the sort of thing they were looking for. The selection board put me forward to the next stage and I was sent to the now familiar environs of Aldershot for a three day mental and physical examination. Once again I was able to prove my mettle and was posted to the Royal Army Service Corps as an officer.

Officer training was fine as far as it went, but I still had plenty of time on my hands. At least I was shortening my two-year conscription by then, so I decided to use any spare time I had to begin to plot out what I was going to do with my life once I was out of the army.

I had a burning desire to go into business and didn't for one moment consider that I would be working for anyone else. It wasn't in my mind-set. My whole family had set up their own companies, whether it was running a shoe shop, a wholesaling business, or leasing a chain of properties. To begin with, the idea of a property business made a lot of sense. There was almost a tradition in my family that whenever anyone had any spare cash at all, they invested in property. My grandfather Philip had started this and amassed half a dozen properties, which he leased out on a philanthropic basis. My father had followed his lead and by now he had a small portfolio of shops, which he too leased out. I'd helped him out on that side of the business before I joined-up. Property was definitely an option for the future, but I'd need capital to buy a property, so I reasoned I'd need to do something else too. Besides, I didn't see investing in bricks and mortar as my only business opportunity.

I was sitting in my quarters, wracking my brain, thinking of what to do when I glanced out of the windows. Great drops of water were running down the glass pane as the rain lashed at it remorselessly. *I am sure my abiding memory of this army experience will be of being wet for half the time.* I thought grimly.

I really had spent an unreasonable amount of time soaked and shivering in some godforsaken field or another in the past few months. Suddenly an idea began to form. What about a raincoat business? I had been following recent accounts about the rapid spread of plastic. Plastic was now being used for anything and everything from Tupperware to toys. Why not use it to make a new generation of raincoat?

That was it. I was going to go into the plastic raincoat business.

The more I thought about it, the more it made sense. Rationing was still in place at the time and, indeed, would go on until 1955. People needed points to buy clothes, just as they did to buy furniture, food, or chocolate. However, plastic and, of course plastic raincoats, were excluded. The material was a by-product of the petrochemical industry and very much considered a waste product.

Another company had already pioneered a method of making plastic sheeting, which they had turned into Pacamac raincoats, and they had taken off as a real craze. They were made from thin grey PVC that could be folded up so small the resulting bundle could be fitted into a jacket pocket. As far as I was concerned though, there was more than enough room for two raincoat companies. It was not as if Britain was about to run out of rain anytime soon, as my army experience had clearly proved.

Once I had decided on my career I couldn't wait to get started. I spoke to my father who said I could use one of his mews garages in a Cul de Sac called Hone Parade. 1A Hone Parade was a fair sized, double-height warehouse building. During my leave-time from the army, I helped dad expand the unit at 1A Hone Parade, adding a mezzanine floor, which doubled the space. Towards the rear of the unit was a room with a very large table, which could be used for cutting plastic. Downstairs at the front was a small office, next to the toilet. That was to be my base of operations.

As soon as I had completed my spell in the army I moved straight into the unit and, perhaps optimistically, called my new raincoat company Raincheque.

My first consideration was how to get noticed. Pacamac had done a nice job, but if I wanted to make a name for myself, then I needed to try something a bit different. *Plastic*, I thought to myself, *what is different about plastic*? It was a completely new material and felt quite modern, almost 'space age'. Even though it was almost a decade before Yuri Gagarin first went to space, the possibility of future space travel was on everyone's mind. *What about a space suit?*

In a matter of days, I had mocked-up a couple of children's space suits out of black and silver plastic. I even managed to locate clear-fronted helmets to go with them. They looked fantastic. I collared a couple of photogenic kids from Lambeth Walk and I exhibited at a trade show being held in The Agriculture Hall, Vauxhall. To my absolute delight, a press photographer took a snap of the kids in their suits. A few days later, there I was, peering out of the pages of the South London Press, with a space-suited child either side of me. Priceless.

I was on a roll now. I could see that the fantasy market inspired people, particularly when it came to children. I made Noddy and Big Ears outfits based on the characters from Enid Blyton's much-loved books. Next, I produced a PC49 uniform, in tribute to the popular radio show of the time, celebrating Alan Stranks, PC49. I even added little felt hats and labels on the front to complete the ensemble. Over time I created 35 different product ranges and I still have my secret ledgers today with detailed notes of how I costed them all.

A couple of salesmen were engaged to do the rounds of all the toyshops in the Capital and the stores snapped them up. In no time at all, I was employing a dozen machinists in the Hone Parade unit. It was quite hard work, taking orders, running the production side and then making sure

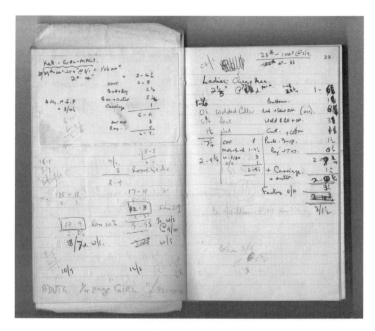

*It looks confusing but my whole business was run
from these pages*

everything went out on time. Even though it was early days and I was a business novice and my expectations were high, I was constantly worried that I wasn't making very much money, despite working two shifts, 16 hours each day.

Then, I had a real stroke of luck.

One of my salesmen friends introduced me to a very nice young lady by the name of Tsang and we got chatting. She told me she was here in the UK to improve her English.

'Where do you come from?' I asked her.

'Hong Kong,' she said. 'I've not been here long.'

'Your English already sounds good to me,' I said encouragingly.

The costing book was the heart of my growing business

'What do you do?' she asked.

'I run a plastics factory. I made raincoats and the like.'

'Really?' she said, her eyes widening. 'My father runs a clothing factory in Hong Kong. He makes anything!'

Now it was my turn to feel alert. I immediately saw this could be a huge opportunity for me. If I could drastically cut my overheads by sourcing cheaper labour from abroad, I might improve the profit (or lack of profit) conundrum.

'Would he export?' I asked. I could see Miss Tsang looked a little confused and quickly clarified. 'Do you think he would consider manufacturing plastics products for me to sell here? We could make some sort of deal and he could ship it over.'

'I don't know,' she said, with a shrug. To my delight though, I could tell she was taking the suggestion seriously when she added: 'I could write and ask.'

We arranged to meet the next day and I helped her draft a letter to her father. I then had an agonising wait while the missive slowly crossed the globe. I didn't get a reply for a couple of weeks or so, but when it finally came, it was well worth waiting for.

'Sure, please send some templates and we will do some test pieces.' Mr Tsang replied, enclosing a booklet with an amazingly wide range of clothing from Lun Hing & Company in Kowloon.

Over the next few weeks there was a flurry of letters and packages crossing to and from Hong Kong. The up-shot was my new supplier could make goods of an equivalent

The Hong Kong supplier provided great catalogues
of their stock

星 光 行

倫 興 公 司

Lun Hing & Company

P. O. BOX 6018

KOWLOON POST OFFICE

Star House, Shop No. 11

3, Salisbury Road,

Kowloon Hong Kong

Telephone: K 675470

MANUFACTURER, EXPORTER
WHOLESALER & RETAIL DEALER
OF

BEADED SWEATERS - KNIT SUITS
DRESSING GOWNS - PYJAMAS ETC.
MAIL ORDER ACCEPTED

FINEST QUALITY

BEST WORKMANSHIP

UP-TO-DATE STYLES

PROMPT DELIVERY

The Lun Hing & Company – my first import partner

standard at a fraction of the labour cost they were being made in the UK. It was possible to make goods with labour costs at about one third of those in London.

Now I had a decent supplier on-board, I decided to expand the range. My thoughts turned to Disney. Everyone loved Disney characters. Since Mickey Mouse burst onto the scene in Steam Boat Willie in 1928, children and adults alike had taken Disney to heart. They loved Mickey, Donald Duck and Pluto, and any piece of merchandise involving the characters was bound to fly off the shelves. I had to make a Mickey Macintosh.

I was business savvy enough by now to realise I couldn't just knock-out a Mickey Mouse mac without getting permission from its creators. I suspected a corporation like Disney would have a significant team policing copyright and would almost certainly demand a huge fee for permission to use its characters. I also wanted to use a cardboard cut-out of Mickey to present the macs. In my mind's eye I envisaged Mickey Mouse holding out a tray piled high with my Mickey Macs.

I called Disney's London office in Pall Mall and explained what I wanted to do.

'Oh, well, I don't really know about that,' faltered the marketing man I was eventually put through to. 'That sort of thing would definitely be done via our head office in California.'

That didn't sound promising. 'Can you give me a telephone number?' I asked, doing my best to sound positive and business-like.

I called international operator, and reserved a call.

Eventually the number was available late in the day so I rang it, fully expecting the trail to run cold.

'Gee, that sounds interesting, why don't you come over and show us what you've got?' said the marketing man I spoke to in Burbank.

That is how, a few days later, I found myself on a flight to America's West Coast. It took nearly three days to get there, with various re-fuelling and over-night stops, and I am sure that many people would have wondered if it was worth going all that way for a meeting that lasted for less than an hour. It was for me though. I took two Mickey Mac samples with me. There was a cute little hooded one for babies, and the design for older children followed the style of a 'proper' raincoat, but with the familiar Mickey look. The Americans loved them. I immediately secured the full rights to make Mickey Macs *and* they insisted on providing me with the Mickey Mouse cardboard cut-outs at no cost to me.

'We will supply the cut-outs,' they said. 'It is our brand and we are the only ones who can provide the artwork.'

'What about the cost?' I asked, doing my best to disguise my anxiety about a potentially huge bill.

'Nah!' boomed one of the marketing bosses. 'That's all right. It's the least we can do to compensate you for your trip over here.'

I could hardly believe it. I wasn't yet 25-years old, and yet here I was wheeling and dealing with one of the biggest and best-known entertainment organisations in the world – and they were providing stuff for free.

Buoyed by my success I produced a television advert

for my range of macs. The year was 1955 and ITV had just launched. It was the first time TV in the United Kingdom had ever shown commercials and it really caught the public imagination. I spent £1,000 on producing my advert, which was a fortune, but demand for the macs rocketed. Joan, who was married to my cousin Leonard (the dentist who also broadcast on BBC Radio), did the music for the TV ad. Coincidently, she had been married previously to my good friend John Trevelyan, but I will tell you more about him later.

It was around about this time that I had an interesting conversation with one of my father's wholesale contacts. George Lecomber had been a regular presence for many years. He was a salesman for a Nottingham-based company called Splendor, which sold sanitary products for women. Lecomber was a real character, tall and thin with a deeply lined face. He was never seen without his Trilby hat and a cigarette dangling nonchalantly from his lips.

'What's all this plastic stuff you're messing around with?' he said to me, speaking with his usual bluntness and confidence. 'Why don't you use it to make ladies pants and baby pants?'

'Baby pants?' I replied, wondering what he was talking about. 'No one has ever made baby pants out of plastic. They are all made of rubber and cotton aren't they?'

'Exactly, that's the point,' he said, jabbing his finger into the air as he talked. 'That's why they are very expensive. Plastic is much cheaper.'

'That's a great idea,' I said, suddenly giving him my full

attention.

'I thought you'd like it,' he grinned and as he did so he rummaged in his briefcase, eventually triumphantly producing a handful of packages. 'Here are two or three pants, all different sizes. Why don't you copy them in plastic?'

I grabbed the bags and began to unwrap them.

'Just make sure they are waterproof though, eh?' he said with a laugh.

I went straight up to the mezzanine floor of the unit, which is where the machinists sat and handed the pants straight to the cutter.

'Can you make these?' I asked. 'They have to be waterproof.'

The cutter turned them over in her hands, examining them by pulling them this way and that.

'It's possible,' she said, with a non-committal shrug. 'We'd need an over-locker machine though to make the elasticated part, and our Redifusion welding machines can weld the sides.'

I was sufficiently convinced of the potential of plastic pants that I decided to invest in the new overlock machines. My sewing and welding team went round in circles for a few days, producing various samples, and when they were sufficiently happy with what they had done, we poured some water over them to test the seal. It wasn't a terribly scientific test, but it seemed to work like a dream, so I pronounced our prototype ready and called Lecomber back for him to guide me on a competitive price.

Lecomber went straight to Littlewoods buying office

on London's Oxford Street to present our wares and they ordered 12,000 units on the spot. It was a phenomenal order and worth a fortune to my company. We could make the pants for one and sixpence each, yet sell them for two shillings a piece. Of course, securing an order and fulfilling an order were two different things. I had to put two shifts into my factory, working from 8.30 am in the morning until 11.30 pm at night for three whole months to get through it all. Luckily the children's outfit work was quite a seasonal business because the toys shops sold most of their stock at Christmas, so we could put that side of things on hold until the autumn, once we'd completed the pants order.

It was exhausting work but, for the first time in years, I finally began to think I was getting somewhere. However, this was the point when I discovered that Newton's rule – 'what goes up, must come down' – often applies to business too.

The day started innocently enough. As always, I was in the office early, seated at my desk which was covered with orders, unpaid bills, invoices and other assorted paperwork. I'd just dealt with a sizing issue brought to me by one of the machinists, when the phone on my desk rang.

'Hello, is that Laurie Marsh?'

'Yes, how can I help you?'

'It's a call from King.'

'I'm sorry?' I was completely non-plussed. Last time I looked our monarch was female: Queen Elizabeth.

There was a pause from the secretary on the other end of the line. 'Will you take a call from Claude Kingsley Rudkin-Jones, but everyone calls him King.'

'Certainly,' I said, wondering what this could possibly be about.

King came on the line and with the confidence of a man who is used to being listened to he got straight to the point. He said; 'I own Blacketts. I assume you know Blacketts?'

I did. It was a large department store group and had shops all over the UK. I barely had time to answer in the affirmative before the caller ploughed on.

'I've seen your macs. I like what you are doing with plastics. You've got an eye for the trends. What sort of margin are you making on those character macs? Do you have your own factory?'

I launched straight into business mode. This was an opportunity I was not going to miss. 'Well, I have a factory in Lambeth and one in Hong Kong...' I began.

'In Hong Kong?' he exploded, sounding incredulous. 'You're importing? That is incredible.'

'Yes, well, it costs four shillings per unit to make them here, but if I buy them in from Hong Kong I can get them for around three shillings including delivery.'

'Remarkable, truly remarkable. When can you come in to see me? Tomorrow at 10 o'clock suit you?'

I obviously said yes straight away. Just over 24-hours later I was in 'the King's' office at 106 Park Street in Mayfair. He didn't look anything like I expected. On the phone he sounded like a large man, but in real life he was quite small and looked rather like a penguin in his dark suit and pristine white shirt. If he was small in stature though, his character was every bit as over-powering as I suspected.

After I showed him the catalogue range of products available from Hong Kong and Hone Parade he came right out with what he wanted.

'You're a bright lad, I'd like to buy your company,' he said, as we sat in his large, oak-panelled office. 'You can run our own-brand merchandise department and transfer your present business to us. What is your turnover?'

I was a bit taken aback. I hadn't expected this. I supplied some information and he said that he would have his accountants check the figures

'On the basis of what you have told me and subject to verification, how does 50,000 of our shares sound to you? They will go up in value as the company grows and you will receive dividends. The shares are worth about ten shillings each.'

I wasn't about to say it, but £25,000 worth of shares sounded like a very large amount of money indeed, particularly for a lad from Lambeth Walk who had barely turned 25-years old.

'That sounds like an interesting starting offer,' I said airily.

The King grinned. He clearly liked to negotiate. 'That'll automatically give you a place on the board of Blacketts. You would become head of our own brand production, I'm sure I don't have to tell you what a prestigious company this is. We've got 20 stores in this country and I've got ambitious plans for more, maybe even abroad. There's room for a clever lad like you on board.'

I nodded. It sounded very tempting.

'And, of course, you'll have an office here, at number 106,' the King finished.

The more he discussed it, the more it seemed like an offer I couldn't refuse.

'OK, count me in,' I smiled at the King and stuck out my hand to shake on it.

The paperwork was completed in record time and my business was transferred to Blacketts. Things continued much as normal, with my factory still churning out macs and pants and some orders still being placed in Hong Kong. The only real difference was I would go to 106 Park Street for board meetings about once a month in order to supply details of my factory output, and would then listen to the King expound at length about his next big expansion plan. After a very short while, I began to think that King was trying to run too fast and my deal was a classic example. A lot of it sounded rather too pie in the sky.

I wasn't entirely surprised when I received a call to inform me the King had been arrested. He'd made a bid for a store group in Canada and done his usual trick of offering shares alone instead of hard cash. The store group had done its due diligence, discovered the shares were fraudulently issued and started legal proceedings. King had been issuing worthless bits of paper for years.

It was just 12 months since we had completed our deal and it was obvious the writing was on the wall. It took some time to come to court and then a while more to reach its logical conclusion, which was jail time for the now deposed King. Blacketts went into receivership and was broken-up in the aftermath. My shares were, of course, virtually worthless. I had lost nearly all my money and my business. I was back to square one.

CHAPTER THREE

Gaining and losing a fortune in just over a year, albeit a paper one, was never going to get me down for long. I was too young and hungry for success for that. Indeed, by the time the cell door clanged shut on the King, I was already well into my next venture. Or, should I say, my next several ventures, many of which I had already been running concurrently with my plastics business.

I was always open to a business opportunity and whenever one came up that I thought viable, I would jump right in. I wasn't looking at anything specific right then. I didn't want to be in clothing, or housing, or any particular field. If it looked lucrative, I went for it. One of my early activities was in weddings. A local solicitor introduced me to a couple of guys who were running a flower shop. A large part of their business was wedding displays, mainly because they had a talented lady who put the flowers together in the most magnificent arrangements. We talked about the idea of putting together a whole package for brides and bridegrooms, from flowers, to cakes, to the entire reception. I invested in a white Rolls Royce, set up links with caterers and a company that made tiered wedding cakes and negotiated options on a number of church halls in south London. The company was called Wedding Boutique and after advertising in various bridal magazines, business was brisk. In fact, it was a hugely successful business for a couple of years, right up until the moment my two business partners fell out and that was that.

I also set up a factory in Lots Road, Chelsea where the head lease of the factory block was owned by Alex Kaye (whom I will talk about later). This was in addition to my own mail order shop in Stockwell Road, which I called Aquatex. The businesses capitalised on the various products being made out of left-over barrage balloons. The MOD, in their wisdom, made hundreds of the things, and piles of them were left over. The materials they were made from, rubber outer with textured lining, made ideal open-air car covers. These products were particularly in demand because vehicles had to last as long as possible in those days. Factories which had switched to munitions work in the war years, were slow to revert to traditional manufacturing, so it was virtually impossible to find a new car. Vehicles had to last and that meant weather protection was vital.

I used the Lots Road factory to make the silver car covers, as well as seat protection covers, and I called the firm Wadey Davidson, naming it after the factory foreman and the delivery man. People would order car or seat covers and we would contact the relevant manufacturer for the exact specification for the make and model of car. It was a very successful business which I ran for seven or eight years until Alex Kaye's lease expired.

In another, completely unrelated venture, I went into business with Laurie Langford to run a gallery in the

London Silver Vaults in Chancery Lane. Laurie and his wife Janey became close friends and still are even today. Laurie and I did a lot of business together, including most memorably, the time when we both took a trip to Belgium and bought the contents of a mansion at the end of the airport runway. We made a fortune just selling the contents of this old house! Eventually Laurie moved on from silver and bric-a-brac and into boats and made a small fortune buying and selling old boat models.

Although I always had many business interests in action at the same time, the most profitable of them by far was my expanding property portfolio. In truth, the seeds for my next business had been sewn more than two decades earlier. Since the time I could first talk I was aware of the family interest in property. On my father's side in particular there was a strong belief that any spare money should be invested in bricks and mortar.

I admit, I didn't put too much thought into it when I invested in a couple of small shops out of the early proceeds of my plastics business. It was just 'what you did'. If anything, I was rather ambivalent about property. Then something happened to change my mind completely.

That something occurred shortly after the debacle with Blacketts. I was sitting in my tiny office below the factory at 1a Hone Parade, trying to work out the best way forward when there was a knock on my door.

'Hello Laurie, am I disturbing you?'

I recognised the man who had poked his head around the door. He ran a small import business and worked out of a unit a few doors down.

'Not at all,' I said, getting up and shaking him warmly by the hand.

'This may come a bit out of the blue, but would you be interested in renting this place?' he asked looking around him approvingly as he did so. 'I'd be prepared to pay, let's say, £100 a week.'

If I was stunned, which I was, I didn't show it. £100 a week sounded like a fortune in rent. For a brief second I visualised the fishmonger shop just around the corner, two doors from our shop on The Walk, which my father and I jointly owned. It hadn't got anywhere close to generating that sort of income.

'I hadn't really thought about it,' I began.

'Well, I am very keen,' he interrupted. 'My business is local and expanding and I need space. I really like the set up you have here, with the mezzanine floor. It doubles the working area and means I could keep all my business in the same place. I could store goods upstairs and have space to work downstairs. My seven-year lease on The Parade is up for renewal. If I had your building I would not need it. How about seven years with a rent review after four years?'

'How about rent reviews every 3 years for a nine-year lease?' I shot back, thinking on my feet.

'Done!' he smiled.

'Let's have a cup of tea in the kitchen over there,' I said, still slightly stunned by what had happened.

While I had leapt into the property investment business, my mind was racing behind my calm exterior.

One hundred a week equated to an income of £5,200 a year. Employing between fifteen and twenty staff and all the overheads which went with that commitment, such as heating, lighting, materials and sick pay, ate into my profits. Here was an opportunity to earn £5,200 a year with virtually no overheads and without having to do anything at all. Being 'in property' suddenly seemed a whole lot easier than being a manufacturer

Once that deal was wrapped up, I started to think about what I could do to take property more seriously. I began to work more closely with my father, helping him with his property portfolio and managing the rental income. Of course, this also meant I had to take over dealing with the bank and to begin with I found this rather daunting, to say the least. Mr Nevitt, the manager at the National Provincial Bank (known as National Westminster today) was a pedantic and relentless fellow. He was constantly on our backs demanding this or that. He seemed obsessed with getting us to reduce our overdrafts. No amount of explaining that we needed to 'speculate to accumulate' and that investing in more properties would yield more profit, seemed to convince him.

'If you don't reduce your overdraft by £500 this month, I shall be forced to call in Head Office,' was his mantra.

At first, this threat used to give me sleepless nights. Head Office? Head Office? What did that mean? I had no idea, but it sounded terrifying. Each time one of his letters arrived I would stuff it in the growing file which was marked 'Nagging Nevitt' and resolve to work even harder to avoid the evil clutches of Head Office.

Clearly there was decent money to be made with the right investment. To begin with, I cast an eye over what we already had in the family. On Lambeth Walk we still owned the drug store and had, by now, bought the shop next door. It was quite a narrow building and nothing seemed to work very well there. After trying a few things, we were then using it to sell stationery and greetings cards and, after leasing Hone Parade, I installed my office there on the first floor, sharing with my father. Two doors from that, we owned another shop that we had rebuilt and leased out to a lovely chap who was married to a French girl. They sold fish and lived in the flat over the shop.

Next to number 180 was leased to a pet shop owner who wanted to use our half shop for storage, but we said no because it produced too many rats and mice. We knew we were a long way from a satisfactory solution though.

How could we fill the space usefully and profitably, I wondered? My thoughts turned to my family. What was it they wanted to spend their money on, I mused? It was hard to judge because most of my loved ones seemed to spend most of the year away from the Walk, travelling. Every time we got together for a family gathering one or other of my aunts and uncles would pipe-up that they were off to Spain, or Switzerland, or the South of France. The new trend seemed to be to earn a few pounds and then disappear off to warmer climes to spend it.

That was it! The penny had dropped. I would go into the travel business. I could hardly wait to outline my idea to my father.

'What do we know about the travel business?' he said, doubtfully.

'Nothing, but how hard can it be?'

It was, as I quickly discovered, a lot harder than I imagined. The leisure industry was in its infancy in the early 1960s and not at all ready to accept small outfits trying to muscle their way in. After expectantly setting up our 'travel bureau' in the narrow stationery shop, we found that both airlines and train companies would steadfastly only deal with licensed operators. As for getting one of those coveted licenses, we had about as much chance of flying to the moon. The only tickets we were able to buy and sell were for ferries, and all the rest had to be brokered via third parties who did have licenses. We managed to sell the odd holiday to friends and family, but it was obvious from very early on that it was not a sustainable business. It was even more hard work than the plastics factory, for a fraction of the income.

'Well, what are we going to do about this travel thing?' my dad asked, when we sat down to talk about it. It was barely two months after we had set off with such high hopes. "There is clearly no money in it.'

I nodded. I couldn't do anything other than agree.

'I think I have an idea,' I said. 'The main problem is the licenses, right?' My father nodded and looked at me expectantly. 'Right now, there are not any travel companies around here, yet we know for sure there is business available. What if we leased the shop to a company that does have the licenses? We can say to them: you can do good business here. If they have the licenses, they'll be able to service an enormous amount of business. This was to be our pitch.'

He nodded and I noticed with some pleasure he was smiling in approval. Not wanting to waste a moment I tossed over a copy of Yellow Pages.

'Let's call all the travel agents listed in there. You start at 'A' and I'll work back from 'Z'.'

We shared a two-line switchboard, so we were able to both hit the phones at the same time. We flicked open the telephone directory, tracing the letters with our fingers to find the right start point. Within a few moments my finger was at the telephone dial.

'Ah, good morning, my name is Laurie Marsh. Would you be interested in opening a branch of your travel agency in Lambeth Walk market? There are no other travel agencies here at present.'

Taking my lead, my father followed the script with the first of his 'A's'.

The first five calls were all met with a curt 'no thank you' and ended abruptly. We ploughed on though, determined to get a reaction. The next number on my list was a company called Wakefield Fortune, based in Central London at 52 Haymarket. A cheery sounding young lady picked up the phone.

'Good morning, Wakefield Fortune. How can I help you?'

'Good morning, my name is Laurie Marsh,' I began and repeated the pitch.

Without pausing, the young lady responded; 'Well, yes, we are interested in that area. Let me put you through to one of the directors.'

I heard a distant click on the line and for a few moments it was silent, save the odd click that told me we were still connected.

'George Fortune,' said a loud voice, enunciating every syllable carefully. He sounded very grand. 'I hear you have something in Lambeth that might be of interest.'

'Well yes, Mr Fortune. We are in Lambeth Walk in the Market. There is no travel agent servicing this area and we believe there is a significant market here. We've already started trading in a small way and wondered if you would be interested in coming to see our operation?'

'That does sound interesting. As a matter of fact, we have a very big client on the Embankment – ICI. We have a room in their building, but we don't have an actual branch. It would certainly be of interest to us. If we could service that client from Lambeth, maybe it would work. I think the best way to proceed is if I pop over and see you.'

'That sounds great,' I said, doing my best to keep my voice steady.

'I'll jump into a cab and be with you at, say, 12 o'clock?'

'Perfect,' I agreed and nodded over at my father who was listening intently to my side of the conversation.

One hour later, a black cab pulled up outside and a tall, thin man with an immaculately groomed moustache got out. He looked every inch the City gent: stripped trousers, black jacket, starched shirt, waistcoat and bowler hat. In one hand he clutched an umbrella and in the other a black leather briefcase. After leaning into the offside window of the taxi to pay the driver, Mr Fortune turned to survey the line of shops along Lambeth Walk. Spotting the small sign we'd put up over our fledgling travel agency, a hint of confusion crept across his brow. Then he broke into a broad smile. By the time I had stepped out of the shop to greet him, the smile had developed into a chortle and then, as I showed him into the tiny premises, he broke out into a full-blown belly laugh.

'Oh yes, very good,' he snorted. 'This is it? Your travel operation? You've got to be kidding me!'

His amused reaction made it very obvious he didn't think very much of our travel opportunity. Having viewed our half shop, which he'd clearly decided was not of any use to him whatsoever, he'd perhaps come to the erroneous conclusion I had performed some sort of little joke for him. Even if that wasn't the case, he was absolutely knocked-out by the concept that I had tried to sell him such a business opportunity in a half shop, which was just a few foot wide.

'I can see it is not quite what you expected,' I began, doing my best to remain friendly, despite the reaction.

'You could say that,' Mr Fortune said, still chuckling. Then, after finally registering the disappointment on my face, he added: 'What else do you do?'

'Well, I am in the property business,' I said, straightening myself up.

'That is good,' he nodded approvingly. 'Listen, this is no good to us, but if you can come up with a property deal where we can both make some money, come and let me know.'

Mr Fortune stepped forward, pressed his card into my hand and then clasped my other hand and shook it vigorously. He then looked around the tiny shop, had one last chuckle and went on his way still shaking his head. I was sad he hadn't liked the travel agency idea, but sensed that something important had just happened. This businessman clearly saw something in me and that counted for a lot. All I had to do now was put a deal together that did grab his attention.

The moment Mr Fortune made his offer, I grabbed it with both hands and started looking for decent property development projects. I reasoned there was little point in looking at the odd shop here and there. He had already demonstrated by his demeanour that he was only interested in something substantial. I began looking at combinations of shops and residential property in good areas. The first deal I presented to George Fortune and his partner Eric Wakefield was a site in Bourne End, Buckinghamshire which had planning consent for eight shops with flats above and car parking at the rear. After submitting my plans to redevelop the area, as well as a viability study, they immediately agreed to help with finding funding – to my intense pride and pleasure. They introduced me to a friendly manager at their branch of Lloyds Bank and in no time at all funds were put in place and a deal was struck. We were in business.

To make things formal, we set up a company called John Laurie Ltd, combining my name with the name of George's adopted son. I had a 75 per cent share in the venture and my partners George and Eric took the remaining 25 per cent.

During the construction of Bourne End I carried on looking for other promising investments. The next one that came to light was another block of shops with upstairs flats in Norwood, in South London. Everything seemed to be going well and following upon the progress at Bourne End, Eric and George were very happy to support me once more. Then, suddenly, during the planning process, the local council decided to pitch in and demanded that we provided basement car parking with enough space for ten vehicles. This was a serious problem. Digging out a basement, with a corresponding entrance and exit, would add many thousands to the cost. For a few days I was utterly stumped.

There has to be a way to resolve this, I thought. I set about doing some research and within a few days I had a solution: a Paternoster car lift. It really was a most ingenious idea. Cars drive onto a large platform and then are hoisted into the air, on a substantial circular lift, revealing an empty space for the next car in another slot below. The number of platforms and, of course, the available height of the lift, determined the total number of cars that could use this contraption. When a car owner wanted to retrieve their vehicle they used a key to turn on the motor and pushed a button to stop the Paternoster moving when their car had trundled round to ground level. Perfect.

I didn't waste any time. I hot-footed it to Derby to visit the only company in the UK then making the lifts. We very quickly worked out that installing a Paternoster lift would cost only a third of the bill for digging a basement car park. Even better, the Derby factory were willing to give me a decent discount because they didn't yet have a car lift in London and this would be a fantastic showcase for them.

The only remaining hurdle was to persuade the planning department to agree to this slightly off the wall solution. I had plans drawn up and then invited everyone in the planning department to visit the factory in Derby to see the car lift in action. As I suspected, the councillors were delighted to have a day out of the office and we had a tremendous turnout. A short while later I was granted planning permission for everything I needed. The second major John Laurie Ltd development was off to the races.

Not everything on this project went quite so smoothly, I should add. When the time came for the official opening of this block of flats and shop units, and of course, the modern car lift, the local mayor himself was invited to cut the ribbon on the development. Sensing a good PR opportunity, he happily agreed to this official engagement and we set up the perfect photo opportunity where he would drive into the Paternoster lift, get out of his car and turn the key, thus sending the official mayoral car sailing up into the air.

Everything worked smoothly on the day. The mayoral car rose majestically and the crowd was suitably appreciative of this modern marvel. That was, right up until the moment the mayor tried to retrieve his official car and the lift wouldn't move an inch. It simply gave an angry growl and refused to budge! There were red faces all round and the poor mayor had to get a taxi back to the council offices. It turned out that he had driven the car too far forward on the lift and jammed the mechanism. It took two days to free it. Still, I reasoned, all publicity is good publicity and all that.

The set-back certainly didn't seem to do my property career much harm. I was constantly on the lookout for newer and bigger projects. None of this is to say I didn't have interests elsewhere though. Indeed, when I wasn't chasing new property deals, I was also managing to carve out quite a lively social life for myself too. Curiously, although my burgeoning property interests were still mainly south of the river, I was beginning to spend most of my time north of it in St Johns Wood.

Henry Kleiman, one of my old Hillel House friends, introduced me to the area. He'd got back in touch with me after we had both finished our stint in the army. He'd been in the King's African Rifles and had spent a lot of time in Kenya during the Mau Mau uprising, and was pretty shaken up by it all. When we met up again, he said he was sharing a flat in Clifton Hill with a young actor called Larry Hagman. It was very apparent poor Henry was not in a good way and I resolved to see as much of him as I could to keep an eye on him.

The flat was a lively place, full of people coming and going. I got on well with Larry, who was a year younger than me. He had a small part in the West End production of *South Pacific* and seemed to be permanently flat broke.

What intrigued me most about him was he was acting alongside his mother Mary Martin, the star of the show, but this was a big secret. Mary, who was 35-years old, had been lying about her real age for years and it was a little inconvenient to have a 17-year old son popping up to provide physical proof that she had been economical with the truth.

After Larry got off stage following the evening show of *South Pacific*, he and Henry invariably used to play poker until the early hours. The flat was filled with a thick fog of acrid smoke from the cigarettes they constantly had at their fingertips, and the amount of booze consumed was eye-watering. Larry was very particular about his tipple, which was always a large pot of iced gin with a teaspoon full of vermouth and a squeeze of lemon juice squeezed around its lip. I kept away from the cigarettes and I had never had a liking for gin, so I drank some beer. Unlike them, I often had to be up early the next morning and I needed a clear head to see off Nagging Nevitt and his ilk. I also steered clear of the poker games. After my upbringing, I could never resist a little sleight of hand with cards and it wouldn't do to be caught cheating by my good friends.

Things were all pretty relaxed between us. I didn't mind one bit when one of my girlfriends, Maj Irene Axelsson, decided she preferred Larry when I took her along to the flat in Clifton Hill. I'd met Maj, who was a fashion designer, when I was in the plastics business. My cousin Romaine had introduced her to me when I briefly toyed with making a more fashionable mac. The design

Up and coming actor Larry Hagman in South Pacific

collaboration didn't work out, but we started dating. I had already decided it wasn't going anywhere though a short while before Larry caught her attention. For a start she wasn't Jewish, so my parents would never have accepted the match. And she lived all the way out in Essex. It was a two-and-a-half-hour round trip to take her home after our dates in London, which was a real killer when I had to be up early for work. I'd never really believed in love at first sight, but she and Larry seemed to fall for each other straight away. They married in 1954 and it became one of the most enduring marriages in show-business, lasting right up until Larry's death in 2012.

In a short space of time, the flat in Clifton Hill became

the place to go. There would habitually be people there most evenings and quite often there would be some well-known faces. For a while it was quite a head turner for an ordinary young lad from Lambeth Walk, but after a short time I became used to it and started to take it in my stride. There were exceptions though. The night I met the three Wiere Brothers, I was in awe of their talent.

The brothers, Harry, Herbert and Sylvester, were well-known for their Vaudeville routine which they had performed all over Europe and in America since the late 1920s. Audiences lapped up their unique blend of slapstick comedy and perfectly executed dance routines. One of their trademarks was a juggling routine where they each threw bowler hats and caught them on their heads with precision timing. Another would involve the eldest brother Harry 'trying' to do a serious number on his violin, while the other two balanced their fiddles on their foreheads. Before long they would all be balancing violins on their heads and in one memorable finale, Sylvester balanced a double bass on his forehead!

In 1951, they were invited to take part in the Royal Variety Performance at the London Palladium, in the presence of Queen Elizabeth and her sister Princess Margaret. There was a huge after-show party and for some reason the Wieres and many other people who performed in the show, ended up piling back to Clifton Hill to continue the festivities. I instantly got on with all three of them and, in particular, quickly set-up a close rapport with the youngest brother Sylvester. We seemed very much on the same wavelength. After that, whenever they were in town, we always got together and I began to travel to some of the European cities they played in too. Eventually, I would regularly go out to America to see them on stage.

In the same year I met them, I had a terrible riding accident and ended up in a plaster cast for some weeks. The Wieres rallied around and introduced me to an osteopath called Stephen Ward, who they said could work miracles. He certainly did a great job and we kept in touch, eventually becoming good friends too. As well as his skill with bones, Stephen was a very accomplished sketch artist and I was lucky enough to be the subject of one of his drawings a few years after we met. Sadly, less than a decade later, he had a very public fall from grace and he committed suicide. He had been a central character in the Profumo affair, which rocked British politics in 1963 and led to the resignation of John Profumo, the Secretary of State for War.

If ever I felt exhausted by the demands of my plastics or property business, the Wiere Brothers were always there to put a smile on my face. In fact, the three of them were real wags and always playing tricks on me. On one memorable occasion, I had travelled to Paris to see them play at the Moulin Rouge. The boys, who rehearsed new sections for their act for at least two hours a day, had introduced a new element to their routine which they were very excited about. They'd spotted a beautiful tall and elegant Russian girl called Barbara Trifonova, whilst she was in the chorus doing The Can Can. The Wieres immediately added her into the bowler hat throwing routine, with Barbara taking the position of a glorified hat stand. Harry, Herbie and

Sylvester did a sketch where one of them would throw a hat and another ducked, so it narrowly missed him, but was expertly hooked up by the next in line. In the finale, all three hats were flung across the stage to expertly land on the 'hat stand'. Barbara ended up with a hat on each boob and one covering her pussy. I was enthralled. She was truly magnificent.

'You have to introduce me,' I begged Sylvester after the show, 'I am madly in love with her.'

'Uh uh, no way,' said my friend, shaking his head and wagging his finger at the same time. 'You have no idea where she has been, or what she has done. There is no way I am going to let you go out with her.'

'That's not fair, can't you at least let me talk to her?' I wheedled, shooting a glance at the stage door hoping she might just walk out. Instead, I was treated to the no-less gratifying sight of a dozen or so willowy Can Can dancers coming out of their shared changing room.

'And you can stop drooling over them too,' he laughed. 'And no, I am not going to introduce you to them either!'

Harry and Herbie caught up with us and Sylvester relayed the conversation.

'Come with us Laurie,' Herbie said. 'I think we've got something you might like.'

The three brothers led me through the busy, night-time, arty Montmartre side streets, next to Le Moulin and along to Rue des Martyrs. We arrived at a restaurant and bar building, where the ground floor was clad in bright red plaster, and made to look like a theatre curtain. Emblazoned above the 'tie-backs' were the words *Madame Artur*.

'What's this?' I said, turning back to the boys, burning with curiosity.

'It's a bar club of course,' said Harry.

He paid our entrance fee and stepped inside. I was immediately bowled over by the sheer number of gorgeous women in elegant dresses who were floating around the venue. Although they seemed to be wearing a large amount of stage make-up, their skins looked delicate, framed by cascades of long curls which loosely brushed their perfect shoulders.

'You can talk to as many of these *girls* as you like,' grinned Sylvester.

For a moment I was thrilled and began looking around the room greedily. Then it suddenly struck me how strangely he had emphasised the word 'girls'. I started to scrutinise the ladies more closely and suddenly the penny dropped. They were all men.

'Oh ha ha, very funny,' I said to the brothers, who were, by now creased-up with laughter. 'I'll get you for this one!'

I never did though. The three of them were merciless teases, but that was also what made them so much fun to be around. Perhaps their innovative approach to matchmaking did have some sort of effect though. A few years later, in 1962 at the age of thirty-two I married a lovely young girl called Liz. Our courtship didn't go smoothly. She was engaged to someone else when I chatted her up at a party and then, after breaking it off with her fiancé, she fled to San Francisco for a while. When she returned though, we finally got together. It seemed like I got my girl in the end.

Liz and I flew to San Francisco in January 1962 for our honey-moon and on to Reno Nevada to spend a few days with the Wiere Brothers, who were the main attraction at one of the casinos. The Wiere's lived in Malibu Beach at The Triple W Ranch where they kept their horses. We visited them there. My dear friend Sylvester had fallen madly in love with Maureen Swanson, a successful actress and a member of the Sadler's Wells Ballet Company. Maureen eventually decided to marry the second Lord Ednam, and when his father, The Earl of Dudley, died she became the Countess of Dudley. Her marriage broke Sylvester's heart and he passed away at the Ranch a couple of years later. I too was heartbroken to have lost such a dear friend.

CHAPTER FOUR

My property and entertainment interests finally came together in 1964, when my property group took over the famous Windmill Theatre in London. By then though, the property company in question wasn't John Laurie Ltd – by then that business was far behind me.

George and Eric had become visibly more nervous with each property deal I suggested, so when I put one forward which needed backing to the tune of more than £1 million, they really panicked. The deal-breaker was the complete redevelopment of a site in Derby's city centre. In addition to the shops and flats that had been my bread and butter for so long, I also intended to build a huge hotel and cinema complex which would be called Superama.

'It's just so, well, big,' George said. 'Why don't we stick with what we all know? It's worked out pretty well so far.'

'Stuck car lifts notwithstanding,' chimed in Eric, chuckling at his own joke. 'No, seriously Laurie, I think we will be stretching our goodwill with Lloyds Bank to the limits. £1 million is an extraordinary sum.'

If I was disappointed, I didn't let it show. I was determined to get this project off the ground, come what may. I decided I would get the finance on my own and started to knock on the doors of various banks. They were all interested, not least because it was a great scheme and I had already proved I had a track record. However, they all insisted that, for a project of this scale, I would need a large proportion of the scheme pre-let before they'd chip in.

'What do you mean by a large proportion?' I asked.

'At least 75 per cent,' came the emphatic reply time and again.

Great. Here I was at the forefront of a huge project and I now had the unenviable task of selling my vision to dozens of big companies before I really had anything concrete to show them.

I called Julian Keable, the reliable and friendly architect I had worked with on the most recent John Laurie project. I really got on well with Julian. Julian produced some good designs and detailed plans and I engaged agents. Before long I embarked on a gruelling round of meetings with any company which might be a likely tenant. It was quite stressful for a while, not knowing if I could get the project off the ground, or get the reward for all my work and investment. After a brief, nail-biting time, I managed to sign up Rank to take the hotel banqueting hall and cinema, Mecca to take the bowling alley and Rolls Royce to rent the offices. Amoco, then a new petrol company, took leases of two filling stations, one on each frontage, and National Car Parks took the lease of the first multi-story car park in Derby.

I kept George and Eric up-to-date with my progress and they seemed genuinely impressed that I had got so far. It looked like we would be able to go ahead, but they still did not wish to be financially responsible for such a large project.

The Derby project was incredibly ambitious, but I was determined to make it work

'I don't know how you managed it,' said George, with genuine admiration when I met up with him. 'Pre-letting those sections to all those huge companies? When did you learn to become such a good salesman?'

'Saving myself from going bankrupt comes naturally to me,' I smiled. I was only half joking. This project really was make-or-break for me.

With the Derby scheme finally on the way, Julian called me with an intriguing idea.

'I think I have a way to help you refinance some or all of your debts at Derby,' he said.

'Oh yes,' I replied. 'Tell me more.'

'Have you heard of a property company called Star (Greater London)?'

The 'topping out' ceremony for the hotel project in Derby

'What, Star and Garter?'

Star and Garter was the nickname for the UK's smallest quoted property company Star (Greater London), probably because the name was so long that financial newspapers simply listed it as Star GTR. I had to confess that was about the extent of my knowledge about the company. It was so small it really hadn't come across my radar.

'I've done a bit of work with them in the past,' continued Julian. 'It's run by a Russian chap called Sion Potelski and his son Robert, who goes by the name of Robert Potel. Sion made all his money in the fur trade and put it into property. Robert is a solicitor and it seems he knew a few people in the Stock Market, so they managed to get a listing for their family property company. There is another guy too, Eric Roland, who used to manage the fur company and he's crossed over to manage the property one.'

'That is interesting,' I said, drinking in the story.

'As you know, it is a tiny company,' Julian pressed on. 'What if you were to merge it with your John Laurie company and take quoted shares?'

Shares, I thought. After my experience with the King, I was not too enthusiastic about shares but I made a mental note to ask Tony Midgen, my solicitor, to ensure that the shares in question were really quoted on the London stock market.

Julian pressed on: 'Working within a publicly quoted company in which you would have a large stake and being a director of a public property company would give you easier access to more money. You'll be able to repay the debt on Derby and then look for other more ambitious projects.'

I nodded enthusiastically. It made so much sense.

'When can you introduce us?' I said.

'Leave it with me.'

It didn't take long to broker a meeting and both Robert and Sion were very interested in what I had to say.

'At present Star and Garter is just about the smallest quoted property company on the London stock market, but if we merge, it will double the asset size and we can take it from there,' I said to them both.

'How do you propose to do it?' Robert asked. 'There's not much cash in the business.'

I liked Robert straight away. He was around 20-years older than me. He was still a practicing solicitor on a day-to-day basis and clearly had a professional business mind. I felt that I could work with him.

'Through organic growth and acquisitions,' I answered. 'We'll choose our projects carefully and arrange funding by pre-letting when we can. We can also use our quoted business and buy companies for shares.

We agreed a deal where John Laurie Ltd was merged into Star GTR. I received a million shares for bringing in the Derby scheme, as well as my other current deals, and became joint MD with Robert. My shares were 'A' shares, not ordinary shares, which meant they would only qualify to be fully registered, dividend-paying shares once the developments were finished. This was the model we would use for all our subsequent deals.

With the deal done, I began to expand my property interests far and wide. One of the first sites I bought as an investment was a property in Great Windmill Street, the world famous Windmill Theatre. The small, 320-seat theatre had earned its fame thanks to its nude tableaux vivants, which were first introduced in 1932.

Theatre manager Vivian Van Damm had developed the idea of putting glamorous nude models on stage, inspired by Folies Bergere and Moulin Rouge in Paris. Somehow he had managed to convince the then Lord Chamberlain, Lord Cromer, who was the censor for theatrical productions in the Capital, that immobile nudes would not contravene obscenity laws. Thus a show was devised around the legendary Windmill Girls in motionless poses and great PR capital was made around the ruling: 'if you move, it's rude'. For a long time the shows were a huge commercial success, even at the height of the Blitz (the theatre's motto 'we never closed' was humorously switched to 'we never clothed'). But by 1960 it was really struggling to compete with the private member strip clubs which were proliferating in Soho. In 1964, rally driver Sheila Van Damm, who inherited the theatre from her father, closed the doors on the Windmill for the final time.

The theatre wasn't really on my radar at all, even though I had seen it when I'd visited Great Windmill Street while doing the property deal on the building opposite. Then I received an intriguing phone call.

'Mr Marsh, it's Tony Tenser,' said the caller.

I wracked my brains. I definitely knew that name from somewhere. Then, it suddenly flooded back to me. In 1949, when I was at Perse School in Cambridge, the Ealing Studios comedy *Passport to Pimlico* was shown at our local ABC cinema. I was already quite intrigued by the film, because I had seen some of the scenes being shot when I was at home in Lambeth Walk.

T.E.B. Clarke's 'Passport to Pimlico', starring Stanley Holloway

Then, something quite extraordinary happened. The ABC cinema manager hired some telecoms company uniforms, sealed off a piece of the public highway and pretended to have it dug up. His publicity stunt, which emulated the theme of the film where Londoners needed passports to enter the new 'Burgundy' district, did not go down well with the Cambridge local authorities and they promptly sent a strong letter to his employers, ABC Cinemas, owned by EMI. Of course, everyone else thought it was a great joke and it was widely covered in the Cambridge Daily News. To us, this cinema manager was an anarchic hero. His name was Tony Tenser.

'You didn't use to manage the ABC cinema in Cambridge, did you?' I asked, tentatively.

'I did.'

'Passport to Pimlico. That was inspired.'

'Well thank you,' he laughed. 'I'm glad you remember

it. Listen, there is something I wanted to talk to you about. I run a small cinema club company with my partner Michael Klinger. It's based in Old Compton Street. We show films that don't have a certificate. Nothing too rude, just a bit sexy. You have to be a member to come in to watch them. I've been talking to Sheila Van Damm, who owns the Windmill Theatre. She wants to sell up. Now Paul Raymond is taking over most of Soho, there is no money in nude statues anymore. All his girls move. Michael and I are interested in doing something with the Windmill, perhaps converting it into a cinema, and wondered if you would like to come and have a chat?

'I haven't really thought much about owning a theatre,' I began. 'I'm certainly happy to come and take a look though. There is never any harm in having a chat'

Tony and I agreed to meet and a few days later I was in Soho, touring the Windmill. It looked pretty run down and in need of quite a bit of repair, but what really caught my eye was the three floors of office space above. I knew this space was probably worth as much as the theatre. If I had to buy it all as a job lot, so be it. There was definitely a deal to be done. All I had to do now was work out how to raise the money.

Even though I had little experience in theatre, I had enough to know it was virtually impossible to raise funds for them. There was no mortgage company, finance organisation or bank that would put up money because it was deemed too risky. I had to be innovative. Flicking through a copy of Estates Gazette as I pondered what to do, I chanced upon a short article saying the Canadian company Canada Life Insurance was coming to the UK for the first time. The firm was opening a London office in Knightsbridge. According to the news piece they were looking for investments. Perfect. I picked up the phone and a few hours later I was inside their brand new Knightsbridge Cross HQ. In fact, the offices were so new, they hadn't even had their desks delivered yet. We held our meeting sitting on chairs but with no desks.

'I know you are looking for investments here and wondered if you would be interested in looking at the Windmill Theatre,' I began, after the usual pleasantries.

'No, no way,' the Canada Life man said, shaking his head emphatically and flapping his hands as if to bat the idea away. 'We'd love to talk about investing in some shops though, perhaps some of them you've got in the Piccadilly area?'

'OK,' I said, thinking on my feet. 'What about if you selected about half a dozen shops, established what the rental value is and then pegged the return on the theatre investment with the rises in rent in the surrounding shops? That means that every seven years, when the rent is reviewed, the theatre rent will go up too. In effect you'll be doing a shop investment, not a theatre one, but you will be helping to finance one of London's best known arts venues.'

This was a completely new financing model which I had just dreamed up on the spot.

'Wow, I've never heard of anything like that,' the financier said, nodding. I could tell he was intrigued.

'That's because it has never been done before,' I said. 'I have just invented it sitting on the floor with you here in your new building in Knightsbridge.'

'I like it. Let me discuss it with my colleagues.'

Without hesitating, he called over a handful of his colleagues who duly came over and joined us on the floor.

'Hey, this is a great idea,' he began, before rapidly outlining my proposal.

The others seemed to like it and fired a number of questions at me. I must have answered competently enough, because after thirty minutes the original man stuck out his hand and said: 'OK, let's do it.'

It didn't take long to do the deal with Canada Life Insurance and contracts were signed on 23 October 1964, my 34th birthday. After that I always said I bought the Windmill Theatre as a birthday present to myself. Less than one month later, the cinema opened with the film *Nude Las Vegas*.

The deal I made with Tony and Michael was that they would lease the theatre and use it to show adult films. The films they showed in the Windmill weren't like the ones they showed in their Old Compton Street venue though, because these had certificates. Meanwhile, I took one of the offices upstairs and ended-up running operations for my forthcoming new cinema interests from there for a short time.

I'd like to say my transition into the entertainment business was totally smooth. It wasn't. In the first year as a cinema, the Windmill made crippling losses. As soon as I could see what was happening I called Tony and Michael for a meeting. By now I knew quite a lot about the industry and it didn't make any sense that we weren't making any money.

'Why haven't we made a profit?' I demanded.

'Well, most of the money went to the distributor,' explained Michael, with a resigned shrug.

The cinema business is traditionally divided into three parts. There is production, where the movies are actually made; distribution, which is how the films are supplied, marketed and delivered by special couriers to all the venues; and finally exhibitions, which is the cinema on the high street that shows the films to the paying audience. For some reason we seemed to have the distribution part all wrong.

'OK, well let's get in touch with the distributor and change the deal,' I said.

Tony and Michael looked a little embarrassed. 'Well, erm, we *are* the distributor,' Michael said at last.

This pair were obviously far cannier than I had taken them for. They'd been showing films that they owned the rights to and, as a result, 90 per cent of the profits were going straight back into their pockets. It was a situation that clearly couldn't continue. I immediately negotiated an end to our arrangement, letting them know in no uncertain terms that what they had been doing was usually termed 'fraud'. Tony went off to set-up a film company called Tigon films. I didn't know it then, but Tigon was going to feature a lot in my future career, but for now I was busy elsewhere with building up the property portfolio of Star GTR and still retaining my interest in L P Marsh Properties.

As for the Windmill, in 1970, after six years of ownership, Paul Raymond approached me and negotiated to buy it. He wanted to move his publishing department to the offices and revamp the auditorium. We already knew each other quite well and saw each other from time to time. We did a good deal: he paid me £1 million, so I had no complaints there!

After our marriage in 1962, I lived with Liz in a penthouse in Laurie House, 9 Airlie Gardens, overlooking Holland Park. We looked down onto vast water reservoirs belonging to the Metropolitan Water Board, just across the road from the Windsor Castle, a famous 150-year-old pub. The water company had also managed to squeeze in an austere, characterless HQ to one side. I often thought: *this site probably provided water for the whole of West London, but why was it here?* That was surely one of the most valuable pieces of real estate in London.

An interesting property play came to me. Digging out my well-thumbed copy of Yellow Pages, I rang the Property Director of Metropolitan Water. After introducing myself and explaining what I did, I said: 'Why don't I buy the site from you? I would move the tanks to a new site, beneath the tennis courts in Holland Park. We could put the tennis courts back on top of them and you'll be able to leave the site and sell it. Afterwards, we could develop the site.'

There was a pause as he took it all in. 'That does sound like a good idea,' he admitted. 'Is it really possible to do that?'

'Of course,' I said. 'In fact, I have already had my

engineers look at it and they say it is possible. Simply demolish the tennis courts, put the tanks in and then put the courts back again on top, new courts for old.'

Metropolitan Water had a board meeting and then they agreed to allow my suggestion to progress. I wasted no time in getting my engineers and architects to draw up the plans. The water company co-operated with supplying title plans and so forth. In fact, they said we could have all the land, once we moved the tanks, as long as we built them a new office block on the site as part of the deal. I agreed to this costly addition.

At the eleventh hour I received a call from Metropolitan Water with devastating news. They couldn't go ahead.

'We're a Public Authority and we have to put this site out to tender,' they admitted, rather embarrassed at bringing-up this revelation at such a late stage.

There wasn't much I could do, so I submitted to the tender process. Fortunately, my own agreement with Holland Park effectively gave me a significant edge and my research was far more advanced than any other interested party. I was able to make an acceptable, competitive offer. Metropolitan Water Board sold us the site at what I thought was a reasonable price and we set about building the 120-apartment Kensington Heights building, which is still there today and now worth at least a half-a-billion pounds.

Now my property deals were growing in size each time, it made sense for Star GTR to expand too. Robert Potel and I agreed to begin looking seriously at acquisitions to grow the group, just as we had first discussed.

One of the companies I had my eye on was Watney Mann Property Company, which was connected to the famous Watney Mann brewer. I had got to know a couple of the senior people there quite well because I had been working with them on a large joint venture in Henry Street in Dublin. Alec Woodward, the managing director, and Stanley Honeyman, the chief surveyor, were introduced to me when I was trying to assemble a large, one-and-a-half-acre scheme behind the famous O'Connell Street, the city's main thoroughfare. Watney Mann had an interest because they owned three or four pubs in the Moore Street Market area, which adjoined the site. Our early connection had not gone as smoothly as I hoped, but this was through no fault of Watney Mann.

I had also agreed an outline tie-up with Arnotts, an established department store on Henry Street, which was really the lynch-pin of the proposed new shopping centre development. Ryan, the local director and one of the numerous family owners of Arnotts, invited me to spend an evening with him and his wife at home and down a few drinks to cement our relationship. I have to say that I had been getting along with Ryan quite well, so it sounded like a pleasant plan. I told my partner Robert about this invitation and he decided to join me. Big Mistake!

Our hired car took us both out to a large, old mansion to the North of Dublin and by the time we arrived it was obvious Ryan had already downed a few. He was a keen horseman and hunter and decided he would show us how he had been training his horse to jump. Inexplicably, he 'mounted' his wife and then, with liberal use of his riding crop, he galloped her about the room. Sensibly, I remained silent, but Robert was so horrified he berated Ryan, his face red with indignation. Well, that was the end of that. Ryan told us to get out of his house, out of his country and out of the deal. We did what we were told and sold the combined Watney and Star portfolio of properties we had already accumulated in the area. Fortunately, we made a decent sum out of it, so it didn't end as badly as it might have.

There was something interesting about Watney Mann Properties ever since its brush with Charles Clore, the property developer famous for developing the concept of sale and leaseback. Some years earlier Clore was very interested in Watney Mann's Stag Brewery site beside London's Victoria Station. Watney Mann owned this huge area of prime real estate, and Clore cleverly spotted that if he bought all their buildings, warehouses and pubs at market price and then developed the Stag Brewery site, he would end up with the whole lot for nothing. That is how valuable the head office land was.

Alec Woodward and Stanley Honeyman had led what was then a very innovative counter-attack by splitting the business into two, putting the pubs in one company and the property in another. Both parts of the newly divided business were listed on the London Stock Exchange, which enhanced the market value of the whole Group. By doing this they managed to create a property company with a higher PE value than the brewery. Although it didn't have a huge valuation, perhaps just £3 million or so, it was enough to see off Clore because he was bidding £3 million for the *whole* company and now just the new property company division was worth an equivalent sum.

After I got to know Alec and Stanley in Dublin, I decided it would be a good time to tackle them about their property division, which had been bumping along doing nothing in particular ever since the Clore deal fell through.

'Why are you keeping that property company?' I asked Alec and Stanley. 'It is not going anywhere. You could sell it to us for shares.'

That is how I was able to negotiate the acquisition of Watney Mann Property Company, an all-share deal. We also got Watney's name on our board which was a huge PR coup because it provided prestige. Here we were, Star and Garter, a tiny property group, suddenly in bed with the Watney Mann brewing giant.

•••

Our next big acquisition was another public company, Rodwell PLC. The eponymous founder had got himself into debt with a huge project to build the New London Theatre in Drury Lane. Foolishly, he had personally guaranteed the scheme and was forced into personal bankruptcy by delays on the project. Legally, he could no longer act as a director of a public company, so Star GTR stepped in with another compelling, all-share offer. Rodwell PLC came with a lovely office just off Jermyn Street in Piccadilly and, remarkably, we managed to recoup a large proportion of the purchase price by selling it off once they'd moved out.

Another acquisition, which came close on the heels

of the other two, was Metropolitan and Provisional Properties PLC, and by now it was clear Star GTR was a serious player. I had come to know Jack and Philip Rose, the men at the top of Metropolitan and Provincial, because Jack, his wife and two boys lived at Cumberland House, Kensington, where Liz and I were now living. I liked Jack in particular. He was a short, pipe-smoking surveyor, around twenty years older than me and a real authority on the world of property. He had even written valuation books which were trade standard. He seemed to have taken a particular shine to me and we would have regular informal chats. I once met him as I came into the block and we sat on the stairs while he puffed away on his pipe whilst other tenants in the building did double takes at us sitting there. I really admired his highly professional knowledge of the property business and, as I felt I had a lot to learn, I listened hard to what he had to say. The Rose family controlled two companies, and one of them, Land Investors, was quoted, but the family had effective control. Sadly, Philip, who was younger than Jack, passed away suddenly and his brother was distraught. Then, one of his major shareholders in Metropolitan and Provincial Properties, Polish royal Prince Stanislaw Radziwill began putting pressure on him to release some funds because he needed cash.

'Listen, why don't you let my property company buy this company for shares?' I suggested, during one of our chats. 'We will underwrite the shares so Radziwill can have his money right away.'

Jack thought it made a lot of sense. He spoke to

Radziwill who agreed immediately and the deal was done. Metropolitan and Provisional Properties had seven office blocks in London at prestigious locations, including one opposite the Dominion Theatre, another in Crawford Street, one in Baker Street and one on London Wall. This was a big deal in every way.

Not all my acquisitions were for the business – I actually bought a house in Primrose Hill from Billy Butlin (seen here on the left)

Along the way, there were several smaller deals too. Some of them were outside of Star and many were quite quirky. In one for example, I had bought a former vicarage and music school at Mount Park Avenue in Harrow with the intention of converting it into two homes. Work had not even started when I received a bill from Three Valleys

Water for £224. I wrote them a polite letter which said:

'Thank you very much for the bill, but you have cut off the water to the house for which I have consent to build two homes. I have planning permission and have awarded the contract for this £550,000 development, but am unable to begin because I have no water. My builders can't mix their cement or plaster or go to the toilet.'

I received a letter back, telling me they'd look into it and shortly afterward, the legal department contacted me to confirm I was indeed right, the mains supply had been cut off.

'Unfortunately, it will be sometime before we can re-connect you,' I was told.

'I have builders on site under contract,' I said.

'How much will you be losing thanks to this delay?' came the reply.

I went away and worked it out and sent them a financial analysis of costs arising from the delay on a weekly basis. It was ten weeks before the engineers came to dig up the road and put things right. A short while later, I received a cheque for £25,000 in compensation for the delay, which seemed like an incredible sum. I certainly wasn't about to argue though. I sold one of the houses on the open market at a good profit before the reconstruction was even completed, and let Beatrice, the widow of my good friend Alex Kaye, have the other one at below market price.

Another of the stranger occurrences was when I

worked with Count Ferdinand Graf Von Bismarck who helped arrange a 25-year term mortgage for us, following his introduction to Banque Rivaud, who agreed to provide interim finance for a massive 60,000 square metre decentralised office block in the Plessis Robinson Petit Clamart district of Paris. In 1972, when we negotiated this deal for Star, the £24 million La Boursidiere development was probably the biggest office block built in the French capital and the interest in occupying it was very high even before it was completed. This immense project, together with Campden Hill and Pontings, were extremely influential in turning Star into a large and high profile player in our sector.

In the process of doing the Boursidiere deal, I invited the Count and his personal assistant out to dinner at the exclusive restaurant at our hotel in Hamburg. It wasn't until later on I discovered the restaurant had sent the bill to him to settle! I supposed they must have just assumed the man from such a famous dynasty was paying. It was a little embarrassing that I'd invited them and then he had been asked to pay.

I was living in Laurie House with Liz, and our children Mandy & Robert, at 9 Airlie Gardens. This was at the top of Campden Hill, next to the Metropolitan Water Board Regional Head office and water reservoirs site. Meanwhile, I had located a ground suite of offices at Cumberland House, which was just a few minutes away, opposite the Kensington Palace Gardens. As ever, I had not managed to get very far from the world of show-business. The previous

FERDINAND GRAF v. BISMARCK
RECHTSANWALT

HAMBURG 1
BALLINDAMM 15
☎ 32 15 39

To the
Secretariat of Mr. Stephen Kornis
c/o Star (Great Britain) Holdings Ltd.

16, Grosvenor Street
L o n d o n , W. 1.

Sent to kelvie (Sten)
4/12/70.

Attached may I send you the bills of the Hotel "Vier Jahreszeiten" for Mr. Kornis and Mr. Marsh during their stay in
Hamburg on November 13 to 14, 1970, which must have been
transmitted to Count Bismarck by an error of the hotel.

Yours truly

J. Seegats

(secretary)

Encl.
2 invoices of Hotel
Vier Jahreszeiten

A reminder from the Count that I had a
dinner bill to pay

occupiers of our apartment were none other than three very well-known stars: Peter Sellers, Spike Milligan and Michael Bentine. The trio behind the hugely popular Goon Show used the apartment to hone their madcap scripts. For some reason best-known to themselves, they each occupied a separate room for their writing collaboration and they knocked holes in each adjoining wall so they could yell ideas at each other. It was utterly chaotic, but exactly what you'd expect from this group.

Fortunately, I had a job-lot of rather wonderful hardwood, wall panelling which I had removed from a hotel in Margate that I was in the process of buying with Alex Kaye. The hotel deal fell through, but Alex let me remove the panelling and I used it to cover up the gaping holes in the walls. I believe the rather grand oak panels are still there, even today.

The Goons were not the only famous faces to come across my radar at this time. I had the strangest experience after my parents decided they wanted to join me in West London. At that time, they were living in a flat behind the ABC cinema in Streatham, and when I offered to find them some better accommodation, they jumped at the chance. I said I would also sort out my aunt Queenie and uncle Mick, because they were living in a sub-basement at the Elephant & Castle in appalling conditions. Casting around, I found the perfect place at Hyde Park Gate, just down the road from Cumberland House. It was a large house, which went right through to Hyde Park mews. It used to belong to the renowned American-born British sculptor Jacob Epstein. The plan was to convert it into flats and give one to my parents and the small mews house to Queenie & Mick for a low price.

Initially, they were very excited and took great trouble over choosing all their fixtures and fittings. My mother was particularly taken with having a green bathroom. I installed a small, two persons, hydraulic lift, so they'd all be comfortable, and looked forward to the time they'd be living so close to me once more.

I kept a close eye on the renovations. It was only minutes away from my penthouse, so it was easy to pop by a few times a week. Each time I visited, I would see an elderly man looking out of the window from the house opposite. I quickly realised that it was none other than Sir Winston Churchill. He was clearly gravely ill and sadly died shortly after my development was finished in January 1965. As a postscript to this story, I should add my parents and aunt and uncle never did move in to 8 Hyde Park gate. They decided against it at the eleventh hour! They moved instead to St Johns Wood.

As a further aside, I might also mention that this was not my only connection with the leaders who shaped World War Two. I had also, by this time, purchased the historic Podenhale house in Surrey, which dated back to the 15th century. During the last two years of the war, General Dwight D Eisenhower, Commander in Chief of the Allied Forces in Europe, occupied the house and grounds, and much of the D Day landings were planned there. Indeed, there was clear evidence of the former tenants, with an underground vault built into the grounds, and telephone lines which went all the way to Whitehall. The lines were cut when I owned the house, but it was quite extraordinary to be so close to such an important slice of history.

But, back to Kensington. One of the most spectacular things about the penthouse at Cumberland House, was the view. It was possible to look out all over Kensington Gardens from the window. Not that I got much time to stare out of the window though. New projects were still flooding in. Star GTR started on a scheme to develop St John's Square in the City with a double-sided office block (and a mews at the back). Closer to home, we took on the task of rebuilding one of the three major department stores which were grouped closely together in Kensington High Street. House of Fraser owned them all: Derry & Toms which sold goods at the top end; Barkers which was firmly targeted at the mid-market; and lastly Pontings, which did all the rest. Pontings was found for Star by Dennis Mosselson, but it was an awkward site (and Dennis was an awkward character, but more of that anon). It ran very deep, almost a third of a mile, and had an underground station in the middle. We embarked on a plan to convert it into a line of two smaller shop units, stretching back to the tube station, with a large hotel behind.

Not everything went smoothly in my final year at Star in 1970. My biggest professional headache at this time was the New London Theatre in Drury Lane, which we had taken over from Rodwell. This project proved to be just as challenging to me as it had to the previous incumbents. One of the conditions of the redevelopment of the site, which had been known by the name of Winter Garden Theatre, was that it was obliged to build a new, large theatre as part of a major mixed development. Unfortunately, as I quickly discovered, the site was utterly unsuited to this endeavour. There were some serious errors in the design, not least that the entrance to the car park cut across the dock doors. The architect Sean Kenny was inherited with the project. He had trained and qualified as an architect and also worked as a theatre set designer, but he made some serious design mistakes. I'm a forgiving man though: his son worked for me some time later at The Astoria.

On a personal note, my marriage to Liz sadly didn't make the course and I felt terrible about it. Her family were, quite rightly, furious and engaged top legal counsel to ensure I did the right thing. They needn't have worried. I was determined to make sure Liz and our three children didn't suffer one bit and signed over the penthouse flat, and our country home I'd bought in Burnham with two acres of land. I worked hard to become a better, more attentive (ex) husband after we parted company. I still look after them all one way or another, even today.

After the divorce, I threw myself back into work, building up my property portfolio here and abroad although, as always, not everything was as straight forward as I would have liked. I fell in love with an amazing hotel called Villa La Massa on the bank of the river Arno in Florence. The magnificent 16th century estate occupies 22 acres of lemon trees and olive groves and the interior so opulent it had been a favourite of many visiting statesmen, including Churchill.

Maureen, a close horse riding friend of mine, introduced me to the hotel because her parents, who retained their home in Chelsea, wanted to sell it and as soon as I saw it, I knew that this was for me. It was beautiful.

I wasn't about to let my heart rule my head though, so I asked some very close friends in London if they'd like to spend six months or so living and working at the hotel to check the books. Maureen's family who owned the hotel followed 'Italian LOW Tax' procedure which meant they kept two sets of accounting books, one for the management and another for the tax man, so I wasn't going to take any chances. The friends, Maurice and Terry Freeman, said they'd love to do it. Maurice was not particularly busy and they were keen to spend time just outside Florence for an extended free holiday, as they saw it.

Amazingly, they discovered there was, in fact, a third set of books! A few canny members of staff were robbing Maureen's parents blind. Profits were actually 25 per cent higher than even they realised.

Once Maurice and Terry showed me the third set of books, I agreed a price and I went away to raise the finance. The banks liked the proposition, but then they discovered something that stopped the deal in its tracks: there was no flood insurance. Worse still, no one was prepared to grant us an insurance policy that would indemnify us against such an event. I could barely believe it. The river Arno was 40 foot below the hotel and had never risen that high in living memory. However, the financiers stood firm and said they would not lend money without insurance. That was that. The deal was off.

The following year, in a freak weather event, the Arno rose 40 foot and water surged into the hotel, ruining thousands of pounds of uninsured fixtures and fittings. I'd had a lucky escape. My fortunes were clearly on the up once more.

CHAPTER FIVE

In the Autumn of 1969, while still at Star, I joined Tony in Tigon Films. We'd kept in touch ever since we'd worked together at the Windmill and I had regularly helped him out with advice, direction and investment. Over the preceding three years I became more and more involved, and during this time Tigon made a series of relatively successful horror and sex films, such as *Witchfinder General, The Sorcerers* and *Mini Weekend*. I had been involved to some extent in the production of each one as an investor, and took the opportunity to learn and contribute to the highly complicated production side, both in studios and on locations. Now the company was making a name for itself, Tony's view was that although he was switched on creatively, he needed a firm hand on the tiller when it came to business. This is why I became a Chairman of Tigon and floated the company on the London stock exchange.

I also brought in John Trevelyan, who had briefly been married to Joan (the lady who did the sound for my foray into TV advertising for the Mickey Mac). John had become a good friend and had recently retired from his post as Secretary of the British Board of Film Censors. I was well aware of John's enormous contribution to British Cinema production for over twenty years and greatly admired his more liberal approach to film censorship. I truly believed that most Hammer Horrors or sexy films would never have existed were it not for his light touch. It appalled me that the industry pretty much turned its back on him after he retired. Apart from anything, it seemed pretty short-sighted because he had a wealth of knowledge. I thought he would be very useful to the board of Tigon and I was right.

The need for some commercial sense was clear. One of the earliest films I got involved with as an investor was *Repulsion*, a British psychological horror starring Catherine Deneuve, which was directed by a new, young, unknown Polish director called Roman Polanski. This was Polanski's first ever English language film and the earnest young man was never short of ideas. However, since I was bankrolling the production, I had to constantly remind him the budget was not as expansive as his imagination. We got into the habit of meeting at a Polish restaurant in Exhibition Road, just behind Hyde Park Gate, every night after leaving Twickenham studios – or Knightsbridge where we were shooting on location. While Polanski was rapidly increasing his English vocabulary, he was not concerned with such small things as funding and budgets. I would remind him of our financial limitations and he would generally wave his arms about declaring that art was more important than money.

'We are running at least £4000 over budget already,' I'd say, while he picked at his Pierogi.

While I generally kept well away from the artistic process of the films I bankrolled, leaving it to the experts, Tony still insisted I had a way with the 'talent'. After *Repulsion*, he would often bring me in when he was getting nowhere with actors and directors.

'Can you talk to them?' he'd ask, as we had one of our many meetings at Hammer House, Tigon's Wardour Street HQ. 'I'm not having any luck.'

The Curse of the Crimson Altar was a case in point. Tony was desperate to get legendry horror actor Boris Karloff involved in the science fiction/horror movie. He'd already signed up Christopher Lee, Barbara Steele and Mark Eden, but there was a feeling that a horror heavyweight like Karloff was needed for the major role. Unfortunately, Karloff didn't share the same opinion.

'He is adamant he doesn't feel fit enough to do it,' Tony said, looking utterly fed up. 'How do you feel about going over to the States to try to talk him into it?'

'The States?' I said.

'Yes, he has a house over in Hollywood Hills.'

I agreed to go and a flight was duly booked to Los Angeles. When I arrived at Karloff's pleasant home in LA, it was immediately very clear why the star didn't want to do the picture. He was battling with arthritis and emphysema and wearing leg callipers, being largely confined to a wheelchair.

I noticed Karloff's wife called him Billy. He had changed his name from William Pratt to reflect his very specialised lead roles for which he attained world fame. I opted to use the same name, to accelerate the getting-to-know-you process. Unfortunately, it didn't seem to have much of a positive effect.

'I really don't want to do any more films,' he said as soon as I broached the subject. He sounded friendly enough. He just didn't want the fans to remember him in this way.

Other than this, the pair of us got on very well and spent a pleasant afternoon together chatting about anything and everything. I had the actor in stitches of laughter when I told him about my experience of National Service as Professor Marsh and all the meaningless tasks they made us do. During the course of our chat, I discovered he had one over-riding passion: cricket.

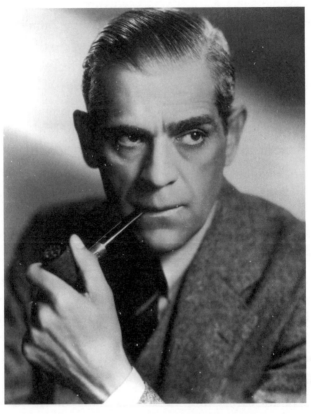

Hollywood star Boris Karloff

'I'll tell you what, I have an offer you can't refuse,' I said at last. 'Filming of *The Curse of the Crimson Altar* is scheduled for this summer. If you agree to come to London, I will throw in a season ticket to Lords throughout your stay. You can go and watch world class cricket any day you are not on set and I will do my best to change your schedule so you get as much time there as possible.'

Billy/Boris grinned, nodded and put up his hands in mock surrender.

'OK, OK, you've got me,' he laughed. 'There is one more condition though.'

'What is that,' I said, smiling too, mainly from relief my mission had been successful.

'I want to rename my character Professor Marsh.'

I was laughing now. The actor's use of my old army nickname was both flattering and quite touching. Ironically, in all the years I was in the film business, this would be the one and only time I would ever get my name on the credits.

While I financed most of Tigon's productions using my Star shares as security with Bank of America, I did my best to stay as far away as possible from the creative process, bar signing-up the odd Hollywood legend. By far the greatest proportion of my time was still taken up with property deals, which were now stretching out to America, mainland Europe and beyond. Star GTR had been renamed Star (Great Britain) and from being the smallest property group in the country, was now one of the biggest, with gross asset values of around £370 million on paper. Still,

I did manage to spend a fair bit of time in Wardour Street to keep an eye on things with Tigon. To begin with, I was a little star struck. It was still a novelty to wander into the office and bump into Polanski, Roger Moore, or Maureen Lipman. I should probably add too, that for a recently divorced man in his late thirties, being surrounded by numerous pretty actresses was quite tantalising.

I never did lose sight of the fact that it was a business though. Like all the other businesses I ran, it had to make a profit, or there was little point putting in either the time or the money. Tigon was making considerably less profit than my property deals, but I reasoned it was a business I enjoyed being part of. So, while Tigon made films that cost just £30,000 or £40,000 and was turning a decent profit, I was happy. However, when Tony began to get more ambitious and began making horror films with production costs in excess of £150,000 or even £200,000, and then they barely made any money at all, let alone break even, I was less happy. Then, when we got involved with big films that cost far more and then lost serious money, I was very unhappy indeed.

What was really frustrating was there never seemed to be any logic to whether a film broke even, or made a fortune. It was very rare to have a sure-fire winner and the only way to even try to do so was get the best possible people on board. Tigon was fortunate enough to work on a few films with the fantastically talented director, Michael Reeves, before his tragic death from an accidental alcohol and barbiturate overdose at the age of 25-years old. He directed *The Sorcerers*, which again starred Boris Karloff, and Tigon's most successful film *Witchfinder General*. Michael was just 24 when he co-wrote and directed *Witchfinder General*, starring Vincent Price, and it has been called one of the best horror films Britain has ever produced.

I was introduced to Michael when Tigon was making *The Sorcerers* and I was still in my advisory capacity. I was very impressed by him and perhaps this was what sowed the seed for me to take on a more active role. Certainly, by the time he was signed to *Witchfinder General*, I resolved to spend time on set to get to know more about the nuts and bolts of the business. I had a thoroughly entertaining time on location in East Anglia in various villages (which had been converted into 17th century sets).

It was interesting watching Michael work. He had wanted Donald Pleasence to play the title role, but our co-financier American International Pictures insisted on their own horror star Vincent Price. On set there was constant friction between the pair, particularly since Michael kept stopping filming to tell the horror actor to tone down his performance. He wanted the role played more seriously.

Eventually, Vincent Price snapped and said: 'Young man, I have made eighty-four films. What have you done?'

'I've made three good ones,' came the oh-so-calm reply from Michael.

It was only once the edit had been completed that it became obvious what Michael had done. He had goaded the most magnificent performance from the star and made the movie a huge success.

The difference between success and failure can be down

to the slightest thing though. *Black Beauty*, which should have been one of Tigon's success stories if you based that on box office receipts alone, only made a modest profit after the most curious incident.

Harry Alan Towers, a former child actor, writer and BBC TV producer, was the co- producer on *Black Beauty*, which was filmed partly in Ireland, with the main production in Spain and a few studio set ups at Twickenham. Production took place in 1971, starring Walter Slezak, Mark Lester of Oliver fame, and Maria Rohm. It was one of Tigon's bigger budget productions, costing £200,000 or so, which is the equivalent of more than £2 million today.

Everything had gone reasonably well. We had multiple crews on stand-by in Ireland to film the birth of a foal, which of course had to be black, with a white blaze on its forehead. The first two foals were not black and when a black foal did finally appear, it required a quick dab of white paint on its forehead. This was all crucial, because obviously, without the correct birth scene, the film could have been held up for quite a while.

When shooting was completed in the South of Spain, the rough cut was sent to Madrid to be processed. Unexpectedly, Harry came to see me at the office in Wardour Street.

'I have removed reel 8 from the laboratory,' he announced as he sat down opposite my desk. His face had an expression of grim determination.

'I'm sorry?' I said, not really understanding where this was going.

'I want £60,000 for an apartment in Germany where I

want to live with Maria,' he said.

I was beginning to get the drift. He was trying to blackmail me. I knew he had insisted upon Maria being cast in the production and he was clearly smitten, but this just seemed too incredible.

'I am in love with Maria,' he ploughed on. 'That is why I wanted her in the film. I would do anything for her. I don't care what happens to me. I'm telling you now though, if you don't give me the money, I will open the tin with the negative and your film will be ruined.'

So, it was blackmail. Incredible. My mind raced with how to resolve this absurd situation. There was no way we could afford to re-shoot the film. If we involved the police, he would most certainly carry out his threat. Yet, if we didn't finish the film, it might well bring the company to its knees.

We didn't have any choice. It made me sick to my stomach, but I paid him the money. The can of film was returned to the processing laboratory in Madrid and thankfully made enough money to keep us going another day, despite this ridiculous bribe. It left a really bad taste in my mouth about the movie business though.

Funnily enough, I was the victim of similar behaviour, although this time in my wider business interests. I had been in the jewellery business with a couple of partners and had a fabulous five-storey building, including a shop in Bond Street, opposite Aspreys; another retail shop in Holborn; and a small factory in Cowcross Street, backing on to Hatton Garden. One of the partners, Walter, known as Wally, took several trays of exhibition jewellery to New Orleans in America for a trade fair and never came back! He stole the whole lot. About twenty years later, I was visiting the Spitalfields Market in which Eric Reynolds and I were partners, when a middle-aged, bearded, gentleman came over.

'Do you remember me?' he asked.

'Yes,' I said. 'You are Wally. What are you doing here?'

'I am now a manager in the Probation Service,' he replied.

Well! You could have knocked me down with a feather. I was so surprised after he gave me the visiting card that confirmed his new role that I did not ask him to return the jewellery. Now and again I do muse on whether his own service should take him into custody.

This was my second unfortunate brush with the jewellery business. One of the directors of Tigon and LMG was Stanley Margolis, a chartered accountant. He died in 2014, in Los Angeles, virtually alone and completely broke, even though I had paid his arrears of US taxes to keep him out of jail. Before he decided to go and work in the States, he had introduced me to a pal of his in the jewellery business. He had been offered a large collection of jewellery in New York and I went with him to see if I could buy it for the Booty Shops. I did so and he brought it to London for me. Then he promptly stole a large proportion of the collection and denied that it had ever existed! I decided that the jewellery business was a breeding ground for some greedy characters and avoided it after that.

The beginning of the end for me in the film business was a project filmed in 1970: *Hannie Caulder*. Patrick Curtis, who was then married to Raquel Welch, approached Tony to get funding for a film starring Welch. They didn't have much of an idea what the film was to be about, proposing either a horror movie, or a Western. Tony had always wanted to make a Western, so chose the latter. An idea very quickly evolved that Welch could be a female version of Clint Eastward's vengeful character known as 'Man With No Name' made famous by the *Dollars Trilogy* of iconic Westerns *A Fistful of Dollars* (1964), *For a Few Dollars More* (1965) and *The Good, the Bad and the Ugly* (1966).

The *Hannie Caulder* storyline was simple: Hannie Caulder is a frontier wife whose husband is brutally murdered by outlaws who then go on to gang rape her, burn down her house and leave her for dead. She then has a special gun made (by gun-maker Christopher Lee) and recruits a professional bounty hunter to teach her how to use it so she can exact her terrible revenge.

I was swept away by the idea when I first heard it. I was fully behind the vision of Welch as the glamorous gunslinger. I even fantasised about a whole new series of Tagliatelle Westerns. Sadly, it was not to be. Raquel was quite simply not in Clint Eastwood's class as an actor. While *Hannie Caulder* did moderately well in the UK, it utterly bombed in the USA when it was released in 1971. Financially it was a disaster. That disaster coupled with the Black Beauty experience certainly dampened my love affair with the film business. Years later, Quentin Tarantino would say that *Hannie Caulder* was one of his inspirations for *Kill Bill*, but that was no use to me then.

Not your usual gunslinger – Raquel Welch in 'Hannie Caulder'

I did, however, take two more turns of the roulette wheel that was film production before finally calling it a day. Both projects came on the back of books which inspired me: *The Chilean Club* by George Shipway and *Cold War in a Country Garden* by Lindsay Gutteridge.

The theme of *The Chilean Club* struck a real chord with me because it explored a subject which was hugely pertinent at the time. The country was in the grip of a power struggle between the hugely powerful unions and the Conservative Government. Industrial action by coal miners had led to the notorious 'Three-day-week' and most people were thoroughly fed-up with cut-backs and austerity. In *The Chilean Club,* four British army officers form an eponymous club where they plot to kill union leaders. I floated the idea with the film director and screen writer Bryan Forbes, who had a house quite close to Podenhale, my country home in Wentworth, and he was immediately just as enthusiastic as I was. I was further buoyed by the calibre of actors who quickly signed up to the project: Laurence Oliver and John Mills both expressed a firm interest. I felt we couldn't go wrong.

While Bryan worked on the script, I set about bringing *Cold War in a Country Garden* to life. Again, it was an incredible story addressing a theme which was very much at the heart of society at that time, as tensions between the Western and Russian Eastern blocs had rumbled on since the Second World War. In *Cold War in a Country Garden* soldiers and their equipment are miniaturised to an inch high, with the intention of sending them into Russia as spies to bring the Cold War to an end. The story centres around their practice sessions in a country garden.

Again, the early reaction was immensely positive and I managed to secure the interest of Harry Saltzman, one half of the successful Bond franchise team with his partner Cubby Broccoli. I met with Harry in Cannes in May 1972, and after reading a synopsis which my production manager Peter Thompson had written, he readily agreed to co-produce the film with us.

'It is relevant during the cold war, plus it is also essentially a spy story and has amazing potential for science fiction input,' he assured me and went on repeating the sentiment several times. 'I really want to produce this film with you, Laurie.'

Of course, what I should have remembered is you never count your chickens in the film business until there are queues of people eager to see your movie snaking in a long line outside cinemas. However, I had already secured the rights on reasonable terms. Then, after a promising start, we encountered a major setback.

Our problems all centred around how we would actually shoot the film. This was long before modern innovations such as CGI, so shooting in miniature presented all sorts of technical challenges. We needed to create a short pilot, but even this length of film took Peter a couple of months which was a lot longer than we expected. The idea was to shoot the human action against a blue background and then intersperse it with shots of 'giant' insects shot separately in the garden. It took ages to work out how to get close enough to film our live creatures without frying them in the heat of the powerful lights. After a lot of trial and error, we settled on a system that used extremely long lenses.

Our other problem was far more difficult to resolve:

Harry Saltzman, my joint producer, turned out to be in serious financial difficulty. Harry had borrowed 70 million Swiss Francs in 1969 to buy Technicolor Motion Picture Corporation from its chairman Patrick Frawley (following a proxy fight). However, within three years, he was forced to sell off stock to repay the loan, while at the same time getting into a spat with his fellow directors at Technicolor who were apparently trying to 'oust him' (according to several lawsuits he subsequently filed). Harry later defaulted on the payment to his Swiss lender. Worse was still to come though. Harry got into an extremely bloody row with his erstwhile partner Chubby Broccoli. Broccoli said Harry had agreed to sell his stake in the company which owned the Bond franchise in 1972, but Harry insisted this was not the case at all. He even went as far as to try to get the Swiss courts to dissolve the company altogether and then, according to newspaper reports of the time, tried to sell 'his' 50 per cent share of the Bond film franchise. Earlier they had settled on an interim arrangement that they did not have to meet during production, whereby one of them would actually work on the next production in the series whilst the credits still acknowledged that they were both involved. This worked for just two of the Bond films and it was clear they were not going to ever get along.

I was not fully aware of Harry's financial problems until one day when I turned up for a meeting at his office in Audley Street to find his furniture all over the pavement. I went inside, stepping aside to avoid the burley-looking men who were walking backwards and forwards carrying Harry's possessions. I found him slumped on one of the few chairs still left in the offices.

'What's happened?' I said, even though I already guessed the answer.

'I couldn't pay some bills,' he said, close to tears. 'They've got a judgement and now the bailiffs are taking possession of all my furniture.'

It was horrible to see such a great and charismatic man brought so low. Naturally, I immediately got out my cheque book and paid off the bailiffs, who with a great show of being exhausted by the trials of life, duly returned Harry's furnishings. I knew then that *Cold War in a Country Garden* was dead in the water. Shortly after this upset, Bryan Forbes pulled out of *The Chilean Club*, saying the story was just too 'right wing'.

I decided after that I would get out of the film production side. It just wasn't for me. If I was asked to describe my time at Tigon now, I would probably say there were hits and there were misses. It was a lot of fun, but I was never, ever going to make any money out of making films.

Cinema buildings were quite another matter. Having purchased groups of them from Essoldo and Rank and converting their losses into quite sizable profits, I wanted to try and buy up my rival's portfolio which was the largest one in the UK. I had a good look at their accounts and obtained details from the Trade Association of all its branches, including the famous Leicester Square location which is used for all the Red Carpet premiers, and it was evident that the assets were grossly under-performing.

I rang up David Puttnam, the renowned film producer.

I had known David for some years from his early days as a small time producer, right through to his short-term executive role in Los Angeles with Columbia Pictures which did not work out. His PA, Linda Smith, was a close friend and she regularly stayed with us at Podenhale where she was a wiz on our tennis courts.

'Hey David, how would you like to join me in making a bid for the Odeon circuit?' I said.

'You bet,' he said immediately. 'We must make sure that includes Pinewood Studios too.'

I made some enquiries with my City friends and funding was available. I prepared a bid but it was rejected. Rank absolutely refused to even discuss the sale of Pinewood and since David was keen as mustard to get his hands on this world renowned studio complex any sort of agreement was never going to happen. It turned out to be one of those exciting but short-term ideas. It was a pity it did not get off the ground. About five years later, around the end of 2000, Rank sold the Odeon cinema chain to private equity firm Cinven for £280 million, which was about 500 per cent more than we expected to pay. Much of the circuit was subsequently broken up and is now owned by several companies. In its new form, with Vue Cinemas as part of the group, it was on the market for £1 billion in 2015.

CHAPTER SIX

My experiences with film had been a real trial of character. First there had been the problem with the distribution eating into our profit at the Windmill, and now I had very real proof that the odds were heavily stacked against making real money from production either. However, I knew for a fact there was potential on the exhibition side. My experience at the Windmill had provided evidence that decent money could be made running a cinema, if all the other elements were left to other companies and properly negotiated and overseen.

I cast an eye over the two main cinema chains – ABC, which was owned by EMI; and Odeon, which was run by Rank. By buying a share in each company I was able to get full access to their accounts and they made very interesting reading. While both companies were making a clear profit at branch level, by the time that cash had been absorbed by their hugely unwieldy regional management and head offices, there was nothing left for shareholders. In my view, the management had taken leave of their senses. Something was going very wrong and clearly needed to be addressed, yet no one seemed to be in a hurry to do anything about it.

I was still mulling this over when I went to Cannes for the 1971 film festival. I never much cared for film festivals, but since I was still in the business (albeit with one foot out of the door of the production side), I felt I should go. On this occasion, I did as I had for two previous years and chartered a beautiful twin-masted schooner, The Melina, which was owned by the Piggens family. Bond star Roger Moore joined us, although he rejected all the hospitality on offer. He wouldn't eat anything more than the occasional lettuce leaf and certainly wouldn't touch booze. He was keeping his body in shape for the Bond Movies.

Then I heard, through the grapevine, that the Classic cinema chain was up for sale, although it seemed that negotiations were pretty far advanced. *That's it*, I thought. *That's the answer. I need to buy that chain.*

I picked up the phone to John Ritblat, whose company British Land owned the 45-strong Classic chain. I already knew John quite well, and not just because we both mixed in the same circles as heads of large property companies. He used to go out with my now ex-wife Liz before we got together. I had first met him many years before, when I was on a flight to Majorca. Less than 12-hours after my phone call, I was sitting in the Conrad Ritblat Agency offices in Manchester Square, London.

I was a little disappointed to see John had not turned up himself. *He's obviously become very grand*, I thought to myself. Never mind, I was not there to socialise. The price under discussion was £7 million. I had already raised a quarter of a million pounds as a down payment and had an offer for additional finance from Greyhound, the American bus company, which had a finance division in Dover Street. They were keen to make some significant investments this side of the Atlantic.

The meeting was quite tense. British Land had been in advanced negotiations with another party and if I was going to try to muscle in at this late stage, they made it clear I was expected to bring something exceptional to the table. The strained atmosphere was in part broken up by the appearance of representatives of that other party, who turned out to be David Frost, the writer and presenter of *That Was The Week That Was*. Frost's representatives asked for messages to be urgently conveyed into the meeting that said: 'Mr Frost is still very keen to buy the Classic chain'.

Roy Kinnear, David Frost and Lance Percival – That Was The Week That Was

My negotiations were, however, well under way. Yet, after sweating away for what felt like hours, Ritblat's people suddenly threw in a bombshell. They wanted to exclude a number of Classic sites from the deal because they felt they had 'property potential'. One of the negotiators pushed a piece of paper across the table. On it was a list of cinemas. At a glance I could see that most of them were in London, including Charing Cross Road, the Kings Road and Baker Street.

'Absolutely not,' I declared. I was not prepared to give way on this one. These were prime locations.

The British Land guys looked a little alarmed and whispered among themselves.

'Would you excuse us a moment?' said the executive who had first shown me the offending list. 'I need to make a call.'

He was obviously going off to discuss it with the boss and the rest of the entourage followed him out, leaving me alone in the room. I thought, once again, how annoying it was that John wasn't there to talk it through. We'd have had it all wrapped up in minutes. While they were gone, I picked up the Classic prospectus and flicked through the details once again. I didn't really have to do this. I had spent the entire journey back from France reading through them and knew them off by heart. What attracted me most to the Classic chain was most of the sites had additional potential, thanks to extra parcels of property around them. I could develop the property and run the cinema chain as a going concern. The books also seemed to indicate a lot of unnecessary and wasteful head-office overhead costs associated with running the cinemas, in a situation not unlike the ABC and Odeon chains I had looked at earlier. I was convinced I would be able to substantially reduce those costs and hopefully run it at a significant profit.

Then, of course, there was the question of the chocolate

factory. Yes, Classic came with its very own chocolate factory which made handmade chocolates for cinema goers. I loved chocolate. Mind you, if I had any samples while I waited in that stifling British Land meeting room, they'd have melted long before the meeting concluded.

After a short delay, the negotiators shuffled back in the room.

'We're prepared to put one of them back in the deal...' they began.

And so the negotiations rumbled on, with them going back and forth to the boss and me keeping my firmly digging my heels in. Eventually, the deal was agreed exactly as it was first presented and the lawyers got to work. The following day it was reported in the *Sunday Telegraph*, which seemed very impressed that it took less than 48-hours from my first phone call to the last digit on the contract. The article said: 'The deal ... shows razor sharp minds in the City at their best'. It added that Laurie Marsh had 'brilliantly quadrupled his profits and put a price-tag on his new company, if modestly computed at a P/E ratio of only 10, of over £5 million'.

What tickled me the most was a quote from John Ritblat, who I had yet to see since the deal was first mooted. He apparently said: 'When property men get together, they can often settle this kind of thing in a matter of hours'.

Once the ink was dry on the deal, my first task was to visit Classic's West End head office to check if the administration side of the operation was as top heavy as I had suspected. Sure enough, I found Classic's office stuffed full with 44 very earnest-looking executives who appeared to be very busy.

'I am a manager of this,' they'd say, when asked.

Or: 'I am the executive in charge of such and such.'

The managers of the individual cinemas could easily cover most of these tasks, I thought. They'd more than likely welcome the added responsibility and it would make the whole operation much more transparent and easy to manage.

I was honest with the Classic team and said there would be significant changes. I suspect they half expected it because they must have known they weren't contributing much. I gave the staff the option of applying for management vacancies inside the cinemas, and also for positions elsewhere in my other companies. It took a year but I reduced the head office staff count to just four, and the ones who were left were also assigned to double-up doing jobs elsewhere in my property group and for Tigon.

'You can run things from your homes,' I told the remaining management. 'I don't want any overheads.'

One of the managers, Brian Gauntlet, piped up: 'If I am going to work from home, I need a fridge. I like to have cold water.'

'OK,' I said making an executive decision.

Brian remained a friend for the next 40 years until he passed away in 2015, whilst still working for the cinema trade Veterans Charity.

Now for the cinemas themselves. Almost immediately, some of the Classic cinemas were sold, including the ones that British Land had tried to withdraw from the table when we did the deal. Thus, the iconic Classic head office site in London's Baker Street was demolished and a modern office block erected over the cinema on the ground floor and basement. My Classic executives decided that the cinema was too small and they did not wish to retain this branch, so I sold it to my cousin Romaine. It was subsequently converted into two, even smaller, screens and made a fortune for her.

Classic also had a cinema below the world famous advertising screens overlooking Piccadilly Circus. This is where my good friend Run Run Shaw came in. I had first met him a few years before (this was long before my visit to him with Linda, which I mentioned at the beginning of this book). I had been touring the world, showing film distributors trailers for Tigon Films, and I had an appointment with Run Run.

When we met he said: 'Laurie, will you help me to find a cinema in a key location in London so that I can try out a pilot screening of my Kung Fu films? I will have them dubbed into English, of course. These films are well established and popular in Asia, but have not yet been seen in the Western World.' I agreed to lease our Piccadilly Circus cinema to him and the Kung Fu films were an instant success.

Another key site was the old Lyons Corner House at the apex of Tottenham Court Road and Oxford Street, which was converted into the first five screen multiplex in the West End. The ground floor was snapped-up by a young entrepreneur called Richard Branson. He wanted to open his first Virgin Megastore and had identified this Classic venue as the ideal site. He couldn't afford to pay the going rate, so after much to-ing and fro-ing, we managed to stitch together a deal. Needless to say, I enjoyed many free first class flights on Virgin Atlantic in years to come.

David Frost was equally persistent, although I did not give in to him on Classic. The entertainer called me personally almost before the ink was dry on the deal.

'I still want to buy the Classic chain,' he said. 'Come to lunch with me at Langans and hear what I have to say.'

I agreed to go, more out of politeness than curiosity. It was a pleasant enough lunch at the iconic Mayfair restaurant, but I had no intention of selling Classic. I had too many plans. Frost made a second attempt, subsequently inviting me to lunch at his home in Knightsbridge, and while it was very pleasant, the answer was the same.

As soon as I was able, I set out on a UK-wide tour of the Classic chain, visiting each cinema systematically one-by-one. I discovered very early on that no one from head office had ever done this before and the shock on the staff's faces was clear evidence of how little contact they'd had with the previous owners. I explained what I expected from them and what I intended to do with the chain. I then added that I would be back to see them. A lot.

I was true to my word. No matter how busy I was with my other business interests, I undertook to make regular monthly visits of the Classic cinemas. I would drive to the chosen venue unannounced and when I arrived I would head straight to the toilets every time. I reasoned that if the toilets were clean and smelt OK, that told me all I needed to know about the management of this particular outlet. If they weren't as I expected, I was not averse to getting on my hands and knees to scrub the floor. It was the best way to show the management that if the chairman would do it, they had better do it too.

On each visit I would take a turn in the shop to sell cigarettes and ice cream and would always pay special attention to our customers.

'Hello, are you a regular visitor?'

'Why yes,' the slightly surprised customer would reply.

'Welcome to the Classic and here is a sweet for your boy...'

At first the management and staff were a little bemused. They had never seen anything like this. They very quickly got the hang of it though and began to imitate my approach. It changed the whole pattern of the business.

I didn't forget a lesson I had learned a few years earlier when I had built the huge Derby city centre development, the Superama. The cinema opened with Laurence of Arabia. Even though it was a long film, at 228 minutes, the distributor was quite insistent that there should be no intermission.

'That's crazy,' I said, when I discussed it with the cinema manager. 'We absolutely need an intermission. People will have been watching all those scenes in the desert, so all we need to do is turn the heat up just before the break and we'll make a fortune selling ice creams.'

The manager agreed with me and did just that. Our ruse worked too and ice cream sales rocketed. The distributor found out about it in the second week of the run and ordered us to shut it down. We didn't care by then because we'd made enough money out of our ingenious plan.

Sales of sweets, popcorn and ice creams are always great money-spinners for cinemas, but my Derby experience showed me that, with a bit of shrewd and innovative thinking, we could make an even better return on sales of these extras. I introduced the idea that we would have a weekly competition among our cinemas to see who could sell the most confectionary, and roped in the ice cream and sweet suppliers to pay for prizes for each week's winning team. The winning teams could scoop anything from a television to a trip to Paris and, not surprisingly, competition was fierce. I refused to commit the whole chain to one of the two competitive suppliers, Lyons and Walls. I negotiated the best deals and, as a bonus, I was regularly invited to join them at Wimbledon Tennis since they both had promotional courtesy tents there. In spite of making them compete on price it was a significant perk that I really enjoyed.

In no time at all I transformed what was a sluggish, uninspiring business into a vibrant, moneymaking enterprise. Our rivals, ABC and Rank, were still not turning a profit. They looked at us enviously and before long came knocking to sell me parts of their cinema portfolio. In 1978, I became vice president of the Cinematographic Exhibitors Association and President in 1979.

My growing profile within the cinema industry resulted in a very curious invitation. Earl Mountbatten invited me to lunch at the Dorchester Hotel in London's Park Lane. I have to admit, this was a little out of the blue, but my colleagues in the industry quickly explained what was going on. It turned out that following World War Two, Lord Mountbatten, in his capacity as Admiral of the Fleet, had gathered around him three or four heads of the cinema industry, from distributors to exhibitors, for lunch in the Dorchester. He said he had a great favour to ask of them all and the thrust of it was he wanted them to continue to provide the latest films and screens and equipment free of charge to members of the Royal Navy.

'I don't mind what you do with the other Services,' he told them. 'Submariners and the Royal Navy are key elements of our society and need your support.'

After a lavish lunch in the lofty environs of a private room at the Dorchester, conversing with this great man, no one felt able to refuse this request. The lunch became an annual and hotly anticipated event in the diaries of cinema's great and good and once I became a significant player, I too was invited into this exclusive gathering. The lunches were always lovely and Earl Louis Mountbatton had some incredible stories to tell.

I got on very well with Earl Mountbatten. He was particularly attentive to me when he discovered I was, at that time, living with Linda Thorson, who was very well known for her role as Tara King in the Avengers.

'I'm a huge fan of the show,' he said, his eyes lighting up in genuine appreciation. 'Would it be possible to meet her?'

Again, I couldn't refuse. As a result, Linda and I spent a lovely, yet slightly surreal, evening aboard Lord Nelson's historic flagship HMS Victory in Portsmouth. The men from the Navy couldn't do enough for us (I suspect they were as star-struck as their boss by Linda) and the service that night was first class. My lasting memory is of the Royal Marine band playing while on their knees because they couldn't stand up straight in the cramped confines of HMS Victory, which had low headroom in the large cannon cabin.

At the third Dorchester lunch, the good Earl introduced me to his protégé Prince Charles. He wanted Prince Charles to take over the lunches when he died. Sadly, that time came far too quickly and Lord Mountbatten was cruelly assassinated by the IRA in 1979. It was the beginning of another good relationship for me. I got on very well with the heir to the throne and was able to help him when he first decided he wanted to have a greater influence on architecture in the UK. One of his equerries got in touch and asked for my help. I opened up the Astoria for a press conference to announce his intentions and spent some time with him beforehand going over what he wanted to say. He seemed genuinely interested and grateful to hear my views, and was particularly complimentary about what I had managed to achieve with the once ailing Classic chain.

In some ways I've always felt a little bemused when people say they can't understand how I had achieved what I did with a business like Classic. It didn't ever seem to me that what I was doing was complex – this wasn't rocket science. I was simply applying sound business principles to companies, cutting out the deadwood and pushing what was left to its limits. Meanwhile, I was making the best of the assets I had and restoring them to former glories where possible. I could have just as easily done the same thing with a company making ball bearings, as one showing films. It was perhaps this train of thought that prompted me to start my own national orchestra around this time – not as much of a radical change as you might think.

I have always been a keen reader of the National press and noticed that a number of national orchestras were threatening that they might have to cease operating because they were so short of funds. *I wonder if they have the same issues as the cinema chains,* I mused as I idly looked-up the addresses of their head offices. Sure enough, each of these well-known orchestras had a prestigious West End address. Yet, I could not escape the thought that there was no need for them to be in Central London paying exorbitant rents. The musicians in these orchestras played all over the world and most of them probably never set foot in those lavish HQs. It was simply a group of executives making themselves feel good, while lording it up in posh West End offices. I'm sure they'd argue there is a prestige factor at play, but if they were prepared to relocate just a few miles up the road to, say, Lewisham, or Catford, the local councils would probably have given them a suite of offices for nothing. They'd have been thrilled to have them there. At a stroke they'd save a fortune in rent.

To satisfy my curiosity, I got copies of the accounts of all the orchestras that had been complaining about funding. Flicking through them, I could see straight away there were a number of areas where savings could be made. I had to do something.

I picked up the phone to the directors of both the London Symphony Orchestra and the London Philharmonic.

'I am in the cinema business and the arts, and believe I may be able to help in some way,' I told them. 'I have seen your comments in the media about the issues with reduced funding from the Arts Council and have identified significant money savings. I wouldn't want to see your orchestra close down. I am a huge fan of music and go to concerts all the time.'

The orchestra men agreed to see me and off I went to their lovely offices. Once I was there they listened politely to what I had to say but immediately dismissed it out of hand.

'We couldn't possibly function with smaller overheads,' they insisted, as though this was the most ridiculous suggestion ever made. 'You don't understand the nuances of running an orchestra.'

I could have, indeed possibly should have, walked away at this point. I certainly had plenty of other things on my plate to keep me occupied. However, there was some spark inside me that thought: *no, I will prove them wrong.* I would demonstrate it was possible to run an orchestra without the enormous overhead of a West End HQ and all the other nonsense that went with it. And that's how the English National Orchestra (ENO) was born – I decided to start my own ensemble.

I enlisted the help of an Australian friend of mine called William Rutledge. He was a cellist and part-time composer I had met a couple of years before. William had lost an arm in a motoring accident and in recent years had taken up painting with his right hand and also tried orchestra conducting. When I explained my idea to start a new orchestra from scratch, he jumped at the chance.

William organised the ENO from home and worked with the number one artists' agency, Ibbs & Tillett, to book freelance performers for individual performances, on a show-by-show basis. We used around 100 performers per show and managed to build up a good reputation quite quickly. We even offered a few talented young freelance musicians (such as Julian Lloyd Webber) their first big break. Our venture certainly intrigued sections of the media who couldn't quite get their head around the fact this mad cinema company director and property mogul was running a national orchestra. William asked Sir Adrian Boult to become a patron of ENO.

Another big name to join us was Sam Wanamaker. He had been trying for a decade to finance the development of Shakespeare's Globe Theatre on the South Bank, where it used to be located next to a Bear Pit. I got in touch with Sam and suggested that I would build a temporary Classic cinema on the Bear Pit site and show a season of Shakespeare films, donating the income to his Globe Fund. He jumped at the idea which I then put in hand and subsequently he joined the board of ENO.

I'll come clean and make it clear now – my national orchestra was not a money spinner. Not by a long way. The box office takings, which are the principle source of revenue for such an undertaking, were not nearly enough to finance a large orchestra and I subsidised the ENO to the tune of around £12,000 a year. However, this sum was peanuts compared to what the established orchestras were losing and I still believe that I proved my point very effectively. Orchestras are not profitable ventures, and never will be, but they provide a valuable service to the community. Yet, while they require subsidy, they don't need a huge amount. They just need to be run on a business-like footing.

As always, things elsewhere in my business were proceeding at a pace. Six months after completing the Classic transaction, I signed a deal to buy the 56-cinema Essoldo Group chain for £4.3 million in cash and shares. At the same time, I bought five more cinemas from the Shurman Group for £170,000 in cash. At this point I decided to put my entire conglomeration, properties, cinema and production, all under a new title: The Laurie Marsh Group.

The deals kept me busy, buying and selling sites to get the best possible portfolio of cinemas. Quite a few of the larger cinemas just couldn't be turned around, so in many cases, I converted them into bingo halls. I got in touch with Mecca, which was by far the biggest operator in this field, and offered them the opportunity to rent the 23 Bingo Halls from us. This is how I got to know Eric Morley, the founder of the Miss World beauty pageant, who was then managing director of Mecca. I got on well with Eric and his wife Julia, and we became quite good friends. He often came to my house and we'd bounce ideas off each other.

One day, he came to see me and told me the Victoria Sporting Club was on the market. He'd left Mecca by then, so was alert to opportunities.

'They've got two casinos, one in Victoria and another in Edgware Road, as well as thirty betting shops,' he said. 'There is another casino in negotiation, at the Park Lane Hilton.'

We both had the qualifications for gambling licences, since Bingo is a licenced operation. This meant there would be no problem securing permission from the relevant authorities, so any deal could be completed quickly.

'OK, let's take a look,' I agreed.

Things moved quite quickly after that. We went to see the casinos and spoke to the directors at Victoria Sporting Club to agree a deal. Our next challenge was to find a buyer for the betting shops, which we didn't want, but we quickly made progress on this sale. Then, at the eleventh hour, just as we were about to sign the contacts, we were told all bets were off. Victor Lownes, of Playboy Enterprises and the London representative of Hugh Hefner, had bought the casinos from right under our noses. He had literally turned up at the Victoria Sporting Club and written a cheque then and there. It was utterly galling, but these things always happen in business. I met Victor many years later, while I was in New York. He seemed like a pleasant enough chap and we spent a very nice evening together in Joe Allen's. There was no point bearing a grudge.

CHAPTER SEVEN

In my varied and wide-ranging business career I have often made decisions on gut instinct: if it feels right, I've gone for it. Most of the time, my gut served me well. Sometimes it didn't. To this day I have no idea what my inner voice was up to when it decided I should get involved with Jeanie Deans, one of the UK's largest ever paddle steamers.

Paddle Steamer Jeanie Deans had a noble history. She was built for the London and North Eastern Railway in 1931. The Fairfield shipbuilding and Engineering Company of Govan, Scotland, which was behind the construction, gave her a shallow draught so she would be best able to ply her trade around Craigendoran and Helensburgh. She was named Jeanie Deans after a character in Sir Walter Scott's novel *The Heart of Midlothian.* Over the years she had a few modifications, such as having her funnels lengthened to reduce the amount of cinder deposited on paying passengers, and the addition of a new deckhouse to provide shelter from inclement weather.

The magnificent Jeanie Deans offered summer cruises down the Firth right up until the Second World War when she was requisitioned by the government and brought down South for duties as a minesweeper and then an anti-aircraft vessel on the River Thames. Although she returned to more leisurely pursuits when the hostilities ended, running the popular Round Bute cruises back in her native

Scotland, the writing was on the wall. Her then owner, the Caledonian Steam Packet Company, was haemorrhaging cash. Paddle steamers were simply no longer financially viable and more and more were being taken out of service. In 1964, Jeanie Deans became another in a long line of these vessels to run out of steam.

The plight of Jeanie Dean was brought to my attention by a small group of men who formed the Paddle Steamer Preservation Society (PSPS). They were passionate about these boats and dismayed that they were all disappearing one by one. While they had tons of commitment and passion though, they had very little by way of financial backing and little interest from would-be paddle steamer operators. Maintaining a paddle steamer was an expensive undertaking and no coastal cruise company was willing to buy and maintain a vessel which ran on obsolete technology. The PSPS group was, however, resourceful enough to whip up some media interest in their David and Goliath struggle to preserve an important part of the nation's heritage against the onslaught of new transport technology. And that is where I came in.

I read about Jeanie Deans' story and for reasons I still can't fully explain, this magnificent old boat intrigued me. Before I had really had time to think it through properly, I got in touch with the PSPS and offered my services.

'I think I might be able to help you,' I told them.

I did, however, make them agree to keep my identity a secret. I wasn't yet sure how this would fit in with my other business interests and needed time to think it through. The more I thought about it though, the more I liked the idea.

My experience in the leisure market made me believe there might be room for an attraction such as Jeanie Deans on the River Thames. I figured if I added a restaurant, a bar and maybe even a casino and/or cinema, I would have a very compelling new leisure venue in the Capital. In my mind's eye I envisioned summer evening dinner party trips as London's Great and Good partied the night away.

The deal was wrapped up in a matter of weeks. The Caledonian Steam Packet Company, which was very keen to get the paddle steamer off their books (and not to have to pay to have it scrapped), let me acquire Jeanie Deans for a nominal sum. I invested in the necessary repairs the 33-year old vessel desperately needed and then put in additional funds to convert it to a more modern leisure facility. In all, I invested £40,000, which is the equivalent to around half a million pounds today. The repair bill turned out to be more than I bargained for thanks to a variety of factors. One issue we hadn't foreseen was that the paddles on the vessel were not strong enough to withstand the rubbish-strewn Thames, which really was in a shocking state back then. The paddles had to be replaced with reinforced versions. Then there were lengthy and costly delays thanks to a seaman's strike. We got there in the end though.

For some 'Scottish' reason, the deal with Caledonian Steam Packet Company meant we needed to change the paddle steamer's name. After giving it much thought I figured that, as her new home would be on the Thames, a suitable name would be: Queen of the South.

The Jeanie Deans, which later became the
Queen of the South

In 1967, by the time we finished the renovations and were ready to launch, the Queen of the South had two restaurants and a bar. I planned to add a casino and a cinema at the end of the first year of trading and intended to get a team to fit them while the paddle steamer was in dock for the winter months.

If I had reckoned upon smooth sailing from there on in, I was in for a nasty shock. I hadn't factored in the Port of London Authority who, as I quickly discovered, seemed determined to thwart me at every turn.

The first time I came across this organisation, which policed all the commercial traffic on the Thames, was when they sent an inspector along to assess the Queen of the South for its suitability for a license to trade on the river. The Port of London Authority's representative came up with every objection you could imagine and a few more besides. Then, after weeks spent laboriously answering, or resolving, each of the niggles and complaints, the inspector promptly left his job just as we were on the point of approval and we had to start the whole process all over again! It was enough to make a grown man weep. When we'd finally satisfied the second inspector, I breathed a sigh of relief, put it all behind me and set about organising a glitzy launch.

Everyone was intensely interested in this new and unusual facility and a large number of VIPs and press eagerly accepted my invitation to the champagne launch of London's newest attraction. I felt a glow of pride. I was never going to make a fortune from this venture, but I had played an important role in saving part of my country's heritage. It wasn't my usual line of business, but it had given me a huge amount of enjoyment.

Then disaster struck and the timing could not have been worse.

The first I knew about it was when I was aboard the Queen of the South with the reception just hours away. The waiting staff were polishing champagne flutes and laying out a sumptuous buffet when the Port of London inspector arrived for his final inspection. As far as I could tell, this was just a formality. We'd already been awarded our license. I left it to the ship's captain and his men to show the visitor round because I had plenty of last minute details to attend to. A little while later the captain came up to me. He looked breathless, pale and worried.

'You're not going to like this,' he began.

What now? I thought. *Surely they can't have found some other way to put a spanner in the works?*

'The inspector says there is a pin-sized hole in the boiler,' he went on, shaking his head. 'It's tiny, I mean really tiny, but he insists we have to repair it before we set off.'

'But, we have more than 100 people coming for the launch party in a matter of minutes,' I said weakly, feeling slightly sick. 'Can't we stick something over the hole and sort it out as soon as the party is finished? Is it really that drastic, one tiny hole?'

'Apparently so. It has to be repaired from the inside of the boiler and that means a four-day job. At least. He is utterly insistent that we can't move off the dock until its done.'

I took a deep breath. The strict drinking laws of the day wouldn't allow me to serve alcohol unless we were off shore, yet we were not now allowed to move an inch. Sure, the party could go ahead on the basis that we were still docked, but I couldn't see it going off with much of a bang if the best we could serve our illustrious guests was tea, coffee or soft drinks. Plus, everyone was expecting a premier river cruise as they sipped their fine champagne.

In the end, the only solution I could come up with within the time available was to hire a tug to pull the boat a few yards off shore once all my guests had embarked. It wasn't quite the cruise they'd been expecting, but at least we stayed the right side of the drinking laws and my champagne didn't go to waste.

Despite the somewhat shaky start, once the hole in the boiler was fixed, the Queen of the South became a roaring success. During the height of summer, it was full every day, making its majestic way up and down the Thames, stopping seven times along the way at places such as Greenwich, Woolwich and Southend. It wasn't making me very much money, but I didn't expect it would for some time to come. The important thing was, we had managed to prove the public loved paddle steamers and wanted them to stay.

As the season drew to a close, the Queen of the South returned to her berth for a few months. I couldn't help but feel quietly optimistic for the year ahead. As always, my mind was brimming with plans on how to make a success out of this venture and I was confident I could make it into a profitable attraction.

Again, I had underestimated the Port of London Authority. If I had thought that the hole in the boiler obstruction was their last salvo, I was very wrong. At the end of the season I received an enormous bill. There were an eye-watering number of noughts on the page. I could hardly believe the Port of London Authority was demanding this from Queen of the South, not least because the sum was many, many times the gross revenue, let alone the profit amount I had made from the paddle steamer over the whole summer – and that's without taking into account my original £40,000 investment. The appearance of the gigantic bill was terrible timing too. I had just spent some time in hospital having an operation on a suspicious growth on the base of my foot. I was hobbling about on crutches and not in the best of moods as it was.

I picked up the phone to the Port of London Authority.

'I need to discuss this bill with you,' I began.

The PLA representative interrupted: 'When we first licensed the boat you will remember that we gave you a contract which set out the terms of your license to use the waterway?'

'Yes,' I agreed, wondering what would be coming next.

'Well, it clearly says that, at the end of the season, we will let you know what the charges are.'

'But that is a ridiculous sum,' I exploded. 'How on earth did you even get to that figure?'

'It is based on the number of people the Queen of the South is permitted to carry and the number of stops it makes. In your case, the licensed number of passengers is 1000. Therefore, each time the boat stopped to let passengers either on or off, it was liable for a charge of £500 from the Port of London Authority.'

'But we were making eight stops a day! I had interpreted the contract to charge per trip, not per stop. This means the company is being asked to pay £4000 a day. The paddle steamer didn't turnover £4000 *a week* in the height of summer and that is before we even think about paying costs and wages.'

I was about to add that our profit for the year was just £27,000, in concessions and ticket sales, but could already tell I wasn't getting through.

'The contract does set this out clearly ...' he said, his voice trailing off.

'This is absurd,' I said. 'I would like to come and see you to talk this through face-to-face.'

'Well, I will put you through to my secretary to make

an appointment,' he said doubtfully, yet still steadfastly sticking to bureaucratic convention. 'There is nothing I can do though. My hands are tied.'

A few days later I made my way to the Port of London Authority's offices in the heart of the City of London. As I stood on the street outside, I gave a low whistle. *I know why they need so much money*, I thought. *This place is a palace.*

With some difficulty I made my way on my crutches to the interview room. The building looked pretty imposing from the outside, but the inside was positively grand. The opulent interview room must have been more than 100 metres long and making my way along its length over a highly polished floor was murder on my crutches.

'Ah, Mr Marsh, do take a seat,' said the man I had spoken with just a few days before.

He was exactly as I had imagined him to be: short, slim built and sharp suited with slicked-back silver hair. I glanced down at the table in front of me. There, with the offending clause neatly circled in red pen, was the contract.

'I won't waste your time,' I began. 'I hear what you say about the contract. It is clear that, due to my lack of experience, I had assumed a charge per trip and you have now made it clear that the Port of London fees are due for each stop, but there is no chance I can operate the Queen of the South as a commercial venture if I have to pay this sort of money. In fact, there is no chance I can operate it at all.'

The short man nodded. Then, spreading his hands wide in a what-can-you-do gesture, he replied: 'I know it is difficult, but it is the same for everyone …'

'I can't see how anyone can operate on this basis. You are charging me as though I am operating an ocean-going vessel, not a City-wide tourist attraction.'

'As I was about to say, it is set in law,' he came back sharply. 'I want to help, I really do, because we all want to see the Queen of the South continue to do business. Boats like that should be preserved.'

'How do I get the contract changed then?' I said, my feeling of desperation mounting. I just didn't seem to be able to get through. 'How can it be made fair? I am happy to pay our way, but only if it is reasonable.'

'The only way to change the terms is via an Act of Parliament.'

'An Act of Parliament? Is that true? How could that be possible?'

'I'm afraid that is the only way.'

'What if I can't get it changed?'

'Then you must pay the charges. Even if you do get support from Parliament, it can't be changed retrospectively, so you are still liable for the original bill.'

'And if I can't or won't pay it?'

'Then we have the authority to put a writ on the mast.'

'Which means?'

'The Port of London Authority will make a claim against the boat.'

I left the meeting feeling depressed and deflated. I couldn't believe that the Port of London Authority could be so intransigent. This man had declared that he could seize my boat and do what he wanted with it, yet wouldn't countenance any alternative strategy to save it. By the time I got back to the office, I had managed to recover most of my usual vigour. In fact, I made up my mind. I would fight this lunacy all the way.

Over the next few days I sent of a volley of letters to every MP I could think of, asking for their guidance and support. The feedback was bleak. Although I had a great deal of verbal backing, the news was the same from all quarters. The odds of getting a Private Members Bill through the Houses of Parliament were about 1 in a 1000. The Paddle Steamer Preservation Society was a great help in drumming up support and Sir John Betjeman, poet laureate and patron of the society, was a powerful and well-connected ally. He roped in all sorts of well-known names to lend their voices to the campaign to save the Queen of the South. The London Tourist board also weighed in, highlighting that the Capital was in danger of losing one of its newest and most popular tourist attractions.

Eventually, despite widespread backing, we had to admit defeat. It was hopeless. The Port of London Authority wouldn't budge and, when I didn't make the payment, they put a writ on the mast, just as they said they would. The move unleashed another volley of action from the Queen of the South's supporters, but their words fell on deaf ears. Jeanie Deans, the Queen of the South, now belonged to the Port of London Authority.

In December 1967, the Queen of the South made her last, majestic trip down the Thames, before her final voyage to Antwerp, Belgium where she was broken up.

It was a complete tragedy and need never have happened. Even years later I am still upset about it and can hardly believe it ended the way it did. One of our most beautiful and irreplaceable pieces of heritage was destroyed for no other reason than the rulebook.

I thought back to my experience with the Queen of the South a few years later when, once again, I was at the receiving end of what seemed to me to be some very poor decision-making. This time, the incident involved my main specialism, property, but the sequence of events that surrounded it seemed just as farcical at times.

I had been approached in 1968 by a bright young South African lawyer called Dennis Mosselson. I was still joint MD of Star back then and had also just taken up the post of chairman of Tigon Pictures. At the time Dennis was working for a large property company called Freshwater, but had ambitions to set out on his own.

'I have learned a lot at Freshwater but it is a large family business and there is no chance that I can ever control the company and earn real money there,' he declared, looking around at my office admiringly. 'I don't like working for a salary. I have decided to resign and start out on my own.'

I nodded and gave an encouraging smile. I always admired any signs of entrepreneurial spirit. It was nice to see other people prepared to take a little risk to make it big. It was an attitude that had never done me any harm.

'OK, that sounds interesting,' I prompted. 'What do you want from me?'

'I'd like to be in a position where I can bring you

projects and get a cut when they go ahead. I've already got a few in mind.'

His proposition did sound intriguing and in the following hour or so we batted around some ideas. It didn't take me long to decide to support Dennis. He was clearly a bright, motivated young man.

Initially, Dennis worked on projects for Star. One of the early projects he managed was the enormous Campden Hill residential project, from which he earned a very significant fee. Another came when Star heard about an important site for sale close by in Kensington High Street; the Pontings department store. The Star board agreed that Dennis could manage this scheme and, again, his fee was very large.

When I decided to leave Star in 1970, Dennis agreed to join me in a new joint venture and together we set up Town & District Properties Ltd, which was run entirely independently from my residual interests in Star (Great Britain). He set up a prestigious office at 11 Edinburgh House in Portland Place, and he got to work right away. Another associate of mine, Stephen Kornis who was running his family business, Industrial Exports Ltd, in London, came to an arrangement to share the offices with Dennis.

The deal between us was very simple: I was chairman and managing director and would provide all necessary funding, and he did all the work. He proved a very capable and innovative manager and rapidly achieved his ambition of reaping great financial rewards for his endeavours.

In 1971, after two years of working together, Dennis

announced out of the blue that he wanted to end our arrangement.

'It's been great working with you Laurie, but I would like to buy you out and go it alone now,' he said.

I was a little surprised. This had never been discussed before and, as far as I was concerned, the relationship had been working fine for both sides.

'What's brought this on?' I asked. 'Has something changed?'

Dennis paused for a moment. I could tell he was working at trying to find the best way to put something.

'Don't worry, I am not easily offended,' I prompted.

Dennis said: 'I feel the relationship is not balanced. I am doing all the work and all you do is find the money. You are already a very wealthy man, so it is not a big deal for you. It doesn't feel fair.'

If I was a little taken aback by this unexpected outburst, I wasn't about to show it. I wasn't in the business of forcing someone to work with me if they didn't feel comfortable about it. Besides, I had enough on my plate with all my other businesses. I was rapidly winding down my final business arrangements with Star (or English Property Corporation as it had been re-named a year earlier) and simultaneously building-up Tigon and the fast-growing Town Markets.

'If that is how you feel that's fine,' I replied calmly. 'I am not going to try to dissuade you. What I suggest is we agree on the appointment of a valuer and find out what the net assets you've put together are worth. Then we'll halve the sum and you pay me for my half.'

'But I might not have enough money,' Dennis said, looking a little worried now.

I wondered what he was expecting. Surely he hadn't assumed I would simply walk away without expecting anything for my investment? I pushed the thought to the back of my mind and stayed friendly.

'Let's first of all find out how much we are looking at,' I said.

Dennis agreed and valuers were duly appointed. After a brief period they came back with a figure: Our joint property company had a net worth of £61,250, which was a respectable figure after only two year's trading. It would be equivalent to just over £800,000 today.

While I was satisfied with the valuation, the news seemed to send Dennis into a tailspin.

'I can't afford to pay you £30,625,' he said when we met to discuss it.

'I'm not surprised,' I agreed. 'As for taking capital out of the business, well obviously a sum as large as that would adversely affect it. I understand that completely. Why don't we work out a deal where you pay me over a period of time? I'll agree to let you retain all future projects. You can carry on and repay the debt on a timescale we agree upon.'

'That seems fair'

The pair of us worked out some terms and our solicitor James Barnett, of Hancock & Willis (now linked with Robert Potel's legal firm), drafted a contract which we both signed and that was that. Or so I thought. I was still waiting to hear when Dennis would make his first payment when a solicitor's letter arrived. It said:

The contract with my client Dennis Mosselson is not valid and legally binding. Therefore, you are not entitled to anything.

I could scarcely believe it. I had bent over backwards to be accommodating to this man and his response was a hefty kick in the teeth. I could not understand how he had the cheek to dispute that he owed me anything at all. I had procured all the cash investment in the business that he had built and now he was attempting to avoid reimbursing me for my risk. I instructed my solicitors to respond with the legal equivalent of: the contract is clear, we had a half share each. If he wants to buy me out, he has to pay me.

Letters went to and from our respective solicitors for the next few weeks. Dennis's position was that our contract was not binding or valid and he was not going to pay anything. As far as I was concerned, this stance completely misrepresented our fifty-fifty business agreement. Just because some clever solicitor thought there was a loophole through which Dennis could wriggle out from paying, didn't mean it was right. It certainly didn't mean I would walk away without a fight. My former partner owed me that money. However, Dennis would not budge and I had no choice but to take things all the way.

I employed an independent legal firm, Thornton Lynne & Lawson, based in Portland Place. Richard Freeman, a senior partner, advised me to obtain Counsel's Opinion which I did. The feedback was very clear – the payment from Dennis had to be paid. It took nearly a year for the case to get to court and then, just three weeks before the hearing date, Dennis's solicitor contacted Thornton Lyne & Lawson and said: 'Mr Mosselson now accepts the fact he has to pay'. They added: 'He wishes to conclude the matter and is prepared to pay the full amount, plus interest and all the legal costs.'

'I don't want his money,' I told Richard Freeman. 'I am so upset and annoyed about this whole thing I wouldn't want to touch any of his cash, not one penny.'

'You don't want him to settle?' Richard replied, sounding a little bewildered.

'Yes, I want him to settle. I will accept the payment, interest and costs, but I want the whole lot donated to the Jewish National Fund.'

Dennis agreed to my terms. He didn't really have any choice. And a year later I was rewarded with a medal by Golda Meir, the then Prime Minister of Israel, for my donation – the equivalent of £400,000 today. The presentation took place at a very lavish ceremony, where I was seated next to Golda for dinner. It would have been wonderful, except for her rather disturbing habit of chain smoking, not just between courses, but between mouthfuls!

After I gently chided her for it she replied: 'I like smoking. If I didn't smoke, I wouldn't want to live.'

My association with Dennis had a very interesting postscript. After I sold my group of companies to Lew Grade in January 1979 (a deal that included my office and house in Albert Terrace Mews, Primrose Hill), I bought a famous artist's studio house in St Johns Wood with a

I was incredibly proud to be awarded a medal by Golda Meir,
the then Prime Minister of Israel

part of the after-tax proceeds. The house was close enough to my then office offices in Great Cumberland Place at Marble Arch, so I could cycle, or even walk, to my place of work. The house had not been lived in for a year and I decided to do some extensive development work to make it a permanent family home. I had only lived there for a matter of days when I peered out of a small window at the back of the house, which over-looked the postage-stamp sized garden next door. Who should I see pottering around in this garden? There, larger than life, was one Dennis Mosselson. We were now next-door neighbours.

The passage of time had clearly not helped dilute any feeling of animosity this man felt for me. For the next few months he disputed everything I tried to do. When I wanted to re-slate the roof, he slapped me with an injunction. If I applied for planning consent to move a wall, he would object. Dennis appeared prepared to do everything within his power, regardless of its cost to him and to me, to be a permanent thorn in my side.

Finally, I had had enough. Dennis was by then a very successful multi-millionaire in his own right. It didn't seem rational or right that he should spend so much time and energy making my life uncomfortable. The situation needed to be settled in a civilized manner.

I made an appointment to see him at his offices at Camden Town. When I was finally shown into his office, I was careful to begin by praising him for how well he had done.

'I've been watching your progress and I'm really pleased for you,' I smiled, doing my best to ignore his obvious discomfort in my presence. 'Listen though, I think we need to have a talk. We're neighbours now and I don't understand why you are acting like this. What happened is in the past. Let's put it behind us and behave like civilised human beings.'

Dennis looked a little dumbstruck. He clearly hadn't expected such a direct confrontation. Once again I saw that familiar look as he worked things through in his head. He seemed to be conflicted about how to react.

Finally, he said: 'OK, perhaps we both need to move on.'

Dennis stopped his antics after that. Our relationship didn't become a friendly one but we pursued an uneasy truce. We even managed the odd wave at each other now and again, as neighbours do. He did, however, stop obstructing the work I wanted to do and eventually sold his house for over £4 million. I believe that he took early retirement.

CHAPTER EIGHT

When I first joined forces with Sion Poteleski, Robert
Potel and Eric Roland in 1964, Star and Garter, as it was
somewhat rudely known, was a tiny property company. It
was hardly on anyone's radar at all, but I had big plans.
By 1970, Star (Great Britain) had been renamed the
English Property Corporation (EPC) and was the third
largest property company in the UK. It had swallowed up
three PLCs, Metropolitan and Provincial Property Group,
Rodwell and Watney Mann Property Group. It had also
instigated dozens of large and high profile developments
in the UK, France, the USA and Canada. Everybody knew
our name and our meteoric rise was much discussed and
picked over in the financial press and among property
circles. I was proud of what we had achieved but I was
also beginning to feel deeply uncomfortable too.

There was no getting away from it, the property
company had changed beyond recognition and I didn't like
what it had become. Even though I was, partly responsible,
I had deep misgivings about the impact of our growth.

Each time we made a significant acquisition we added
new members to our board. From a time when it was a
boardroom of three (Robert's father had retired), where we
kicked around ideas and then instantly made a decision,
we now had a top table of 23 people. Each of these senior
business people naturally wanted to make their mark and

wanted time to discuss and digest matters in full. In a short space of time decision-making slowed to a glacial speed and projects which relied on a quick turnaround began to drift alarmingly.

I had been party to the creation of a monster company. There was no easy solution either. Once people were appointed to the board, we couldn't very well demote them. They had just as much right to be there as we did.

We already had to make a number of changes to accommodate our burgeoning senior team. When I first joined Star GTR, we had a small suite of offices at 4 Curzon Place, just off the Hyde Park end of Curzon Street. Indeed, the main offices overlooked Hyde Park. Robert, who had expanded his legal practice, also used the offices for this other interest.

The location was perfect for me. I had always objected to commuting. I could walk across the park each day, from my flat in Cumberland House, Kensington. I used to love that fifteen-minute walk. As well as clearing my head, I was presented with the daily opportunity to observe the changing seasons and enjoy one of London's finest spaces.

After a couple of years, as the company expanded, it was clear we couldn't stay in the same premises, so I found new, prestige offices at 16 Grosvenor Street, a little further North East. It was a nice enough building, with a wide entrance hall and a large car park to the rear in a mews, but it also symbolised the change we were undergoing. I now had to drive to work because it was a 40-minute walk, which was a bit too far. It wasn't a long commute by car, perhaps just ten minutes or so, but it took something away from me. That precious 15-minute downtime in the park I had always enjoyed was gone.

Looking around me at the expanding company, I could see there were some ways we were using our resources well – and some where we most certainly weren't. On the plus side, our very talented accountant David Llewellyn had instigated the installation of a huge computer in the basement. It was one of the very first computers owned by a private company in the capital and it was used very effectively to manage a database of our properties. Right then, all our rival property companies employed costly managing agents to look after their estates, but this machine made us completely independent. We saved 10 per cent gross revenue this way. This was the perfect use of Star's capital.

There was also, however, a worrying side to the way we invested our money. In my view the senior team were far too keen on receiving shares and bonuses. We were also paying quite high head office expenses, rather than reinvesting our income into the future of the company. I objected to the string of expensive cars streaming out of the car park at the end of each day. My early days in The Walk had become embedded in my psyche and I did not find it easy to accept this opulent business life-style.

I should probably make a confession here. From the time I joined the company, my Star contract allowed me the advantage of a car and chauffeur, but I could never quite bring myself to take up this perk. Then, one day, something came over me. *Why was I still running my old motor car*, I thought? *Why shouldn't I have the best?*

For a moment I began to dwell on my own mortality. I could be knocked down and killed any minute on London's busy roads and then it would be all too late. *Didn't I deserve one moment of supreme indulgence in my lifetime?* On impulse, I walked into the Rolls Royce car showroom in Berkeley Square and bought a Rolls Royce. It was a drop-head Silver Shadow with a price tag of £13,000. When I signed the paperwork I fully intended to put it down to one of my companies, most probably Star, but the moment I left the showroom I knew I couldn't do it. I hated myself for what I had just done. I ended up paying for it myself and rarely used the thing. On the plus side, the Rolls probably saved the life of Tony Tenser and his wife Diane a couple of years later. His car was being serviced and, since I barely ever used the Rolls, I loaned it to him. A Jaguar ran out of control and hit the Rolls almost head-on on the wrong side of a country road. The Jaguar driver was killed outright, but Tony and Diane were unharmed, save for Diane's lapdog peeing on her.

It was at this point that I began utilising the services of Tom, the doorman to our Grosvenor Street office. Or, more correctly, the services of his vehicle; a rather fine Vespa scooter. I bought a helmet and Tom drove me around on the only chauffeur driven Vespa in London. I used it to zip around Central London whenever I needed to go to site meetings. It was my way of rebelling against the incessant discussions about bonuses and the fact people were clearly making much more money than they needed. I'm not sure anyone really got the point, or perhaps they chose not to, dismissing it as one of my eccentricities.

I tried, on a practical level, to do things that would keep Star GB/English Property Corporation as sprightly and innovative as when we first started. To ease the log jam created by the unwieldy board of 23-executives, we instigated the introduction of a sub board. The sub board was made up of me, Robert, David Llewellyn and Paul Marber, a talented property professional. The four of us would effectively agree the agendas, discussing the viability of projects, making sure existing ones were proceeding as planned and identifying potential new partners. After we'd covered each point off, we'd vote and Robert as chairman had the casting vote. Then, once we had worked out the most profitable and effective way forward for each element of the business, we would present it to the main board in a wholly digestible way for them to discuss and agree.

That was the plan anyhow.

We quickly discovered that, even when we had done all the hard work ahead of the main board meetings, the large committee of board members still insisted on dissecting each decision we made and discussing them ad infinitum. I could no longer bear sitting in on the main board meetings.

The final straw for me was when Robert & David introduced an electronic microphone system into the large boardroom. Anyone wishing to speak had to push a button on the table in front of them, which would alert Robert, the chairman, to their intention. Robert would then point to various button pushers in turn to let them speak and the meeting would rumble on.

'That's it for me,' I told Robert soon after this device

was first introduced. 'We've both worked hard to build up this company and the thought that I have to press a button to request to speak at my own board meeting is just too much.'

Robert nodded. He already knew how frustrated I was at how things were turning out. We'd discussed it often enough at the sub board meetings.

'Star is becoming like an institution,' I ploughed on. 'I have always worked in an entrepreneurial fashion, making decisions for better or for worse. The reason this company grew so quickly is because we were agile and nimble on our feet. Whenever any of us saw an opportunity we could jump at it. We'd be all over it before our competitors had even realised there was an opportunity at all. What do we have today? Probably one of the biggest committees in the FTSE and an absurd push-button-to-speak system.'

Robert raised his hands, palm upwards, in a 'what can we do' gesture. He was less frustrated than I was, partly because he was always a little removed from the business. He was still a practicing lawyer and since the company had grown so much, as far as he was concerned life was great.

'I'm not enjoying it any more,' I continued. I knew what I wanted to say, but it was difficult to articulate it. Robert and I had worked together for more than six years and we'd been through a lot building up Star and creating the English Property Corporation. Finally, I came straight out with it. 'I want to move on.'

Robert looked up sharply. He clearly hadn't been expecting this.

'Are you sure?' he said. 'If it is the microphone system, we'll get rid of it ...'

'No, it is more than that. I've been thinking about it for a while. I've got a lot on my plate with Tigon and the Cinemas, not to mention my other property interests. I've always followed a philosophy that when it stops being fun, it is time to move on. That time has come.'

Robert nodded again. He could see my mind was made up but it was obvious by his body language he wasn't happy with the decision.

'It's such a huge shame Laurie,' he said. 'We've come such a long way together. When I retire, you will become chairman.'

I let that roll over me. After all, Robert's son Stephen had just joined the company so there was no real way of knowing what the future held.

'There is nothing to suggest you won't keep growing,' I said. 'I'm only resigning as joint MD, which means I won't have a day-to-day role. I will still have shares in the company though. I shall continue to take an interest in the large projects that I have brought in and which are on-going, even after I have quit the board. You can call on me any time if you need me.'

Sadly, though, things did change for English Property Corporation after that. In fact, they changed almost immediately. Once my departure was officially announced, the bank insisted on appointing a nominee to the sub board. From a situation where Robert could always rely on having me as an ally beside him, he went to one where the banker questioned every single move in minute detail and was unwilling to give his backing to anything deemed the least bit risky. It's amazing how much one man can change the outlook and behaviour of a group, but this one did overnight. Robert had to spend hours trying to persuade him to vote one way or another and, thanks to the banker's reserved nature, project after project was canned. Even developments we had previously discussed, such as a massive 1,000 apartment complex in Baker Street, hit the buffers and ground to an immediate halt. (Somewhat frustratingly, another developer subsequently took up the reigns and made a fortune out of this project).

The company continued to expand for another couple of years, mainly living off past glories. Then, during the 1973 oil crisis (Arab oil producers imposed an embargo and sent the world economies into a tailspin), English Property Corporation's day of reckoning arrived. The company bankers took a closer look, declared the company was over-geared and called in various loans. It was a disaster because the group had no way of paying them in the time specified. The only alternative was to break-up English Property Corporation and sell off the most profitable parts to pay off the loans.

I took the demise of English Property Corporation quite badly. I had been extremely fond of the company and proud of the way we had built it up. It affected me financially too, because I still had about one million shares, which plunged in value when the company was dismantled. I had been using them as security for funding films. However, the emotional impact was far more wide ranging. When I had originally announced my intention to leave, David Llewellyn sent me a note. It simply said: 'Please don't leave. It will break up the company.'

He'd been proved 100 per cent right and I couldn't help but feel responsible.

At least I did the right thing by Robert. A couple of years earlier we had made a private investment and jointly purchased a hilltop site over-looking Cannes, where we built a small apartment building. Our profit was represented by the top floor penthouse which we owned 50/50. The penthouse had no debt, the sales of the other seven units had cleared the costs. When I resigned from English Property Corporation, Robert asked if he could buy my half interest because he fancied retiring there one day. I let him have it for £17,500, the 50 per cent cash equity we had both originally invested to buy the land from the Swiss Red Cross. By the time the development was completed, the penthouse apartment was worth about £150,000. Robert and his wife Lisel moved into the penthouse and lived there for a large part of each year. Later, they sold their house in Totteridge Lane, London and spent a lot more time in the South of France. A few years on, he sold the Le Cannet penthouse for the equivalent of about half-a-million pounds and bought an apartment right on the coast with the proceeds. He was, at least, guaranteed a very comfortable retirement.

The year English Property Corporation was broken up was a pivotal point in my career in many ways. In 1973,

I got together with the playwright producer, director and actor Ray Cooney.

Ray, along with his co-author John Chapman, had written a successful comedy called *Not Now, Darling*. The farce, which centred on a fur coat shop in central London, had opened at the Richmond Theatre and transferred to a West End run starring Donald Sinden, Bernard Cribbins and Ann Sidney. Following on from this success, Ray was keen to make *Not Now, Darling* into a film and that's where I came in. He had been scouting around in Wardour Street to find a production company, and he approached me to see if I might be interested in investing in getting the play to the big screen. It just so happened that this approach coincided with an interesting new development in film technology: Multivista.

Multivista was a technical invention of the BBC who were starting to make films using tape instead of celluloid, but were stopped in their tracks by their unions. The BBC wrote off a vast amount of research money and I was able to buy the equipment for next to nothing. This system used TV crews who had adapted to fast filming and worked much more flexibly than their counterparts in cinema. The relevant unions were infamous for restricting their members from crossing over to other trades. The Multivista pilot film trials I initiated were successful – films were edited as they were being filmed, and a very expensive production system could be made more cost efficient.

I mentioned it as a solution to Ray and he, not surprisingly, jumped at the chance.

Even with the benefit of Multivista, the budget for the

film version of *Not Now, Darling*, was still pretty tight. Indeed, many of the stars, which included Leslie Phillips, Joan Sims and Barbara Windsor, agreed to defer their fees to keep the budget down, on a promise of a later share of profits. (Leslie Phillips used to call me up every few months after that to see if it had earned out! I kept having to tell him no one would get anything until the cost of the production was recouped.)

'Not Now, Darling' was a great example of the success of Multi Vista

Although *Not Now, Darling* didn't make a huge amount of money, it was by no means a flop. More importantly though, it proved how well Multivista could work. I was inspired. To me, this was the future. The experience of translating *Not Now, Darling* from a theatre play into a film for cinema got me thinking. There was a clear opportunity to make a series of films based on popular theatre shows of the time.

Just as this idea was percolating in my brain, I ran into my old Perse School chum Peter Hall. By now Peter had very much fulfilled his obvious early potential in the dramatic arts, and indeed had founded the Royal Shakespeare Company more than a decade before in 1960. He was feted by the Establishment for his accomplishments and had already been appointed Commander of the Order of the British Empire in 1963 (he was knighted in 1977). When we met up again I told him all about the success of Multivista and *Not Now, Darling* and suggested there may be a way we could work together.

'Imagine recording some of the RSC productions for posterity,' I urged him. 'Right now, these incredible talents such as Laurence Olivier, John Gielgud and Ralph Richardson are giving all these amazing performances night after night, but in a few years' time their amazing performances will have been lost for ever. If the plays are committed to video though, they can be enjoyed for generations to come.'

I saw to my pleasure Peter was nodding with enthusiasm. 'It's not just the RSC either, there are plenty of other productions that shouldn't be lost,' he said, his eyes bright with excitement.

'I agree. I've certainly been thinking about the Royal Ballet and the Royal Opera. It wouldn't take a huge investment to produce a series of compelling films using Multi Vista.'

I realized that Peter was becoming really enthusiastic about the future potential of creating really important archive Multivista recorded tapes of RSC and Royal Ballet performances with the stars of the day and in due course, of the National Theatre. He even asked me to make a short pilot about his home village, Akenfield, which I was very happy to do.

A still from the Akenfield project I developed for Peter Hall

I had indeed been thinking a lot about a way to preserve productions. By a strange quirk of fate, one of the perks I had inherited at Star was rights to the Owners Box which adjoined the Royal Box at the Royal Opera House in Covent Garden. One of the companies we bought as we built the business up was called Second Covent Garden Company, because it was involved in the second phase of rebuilding Covent Garden and making it into the world renowned destination it is today. The Second Covent Garden Company retained the Owners Box and I made very good use of it. In fact, I often found myself sitting within a few feet of Her Majesty the Queen and Prince Philip as we all enjoyed the latest production at the Royal Opera House. I became quite close to some of the principle dancers of the time, most notably Antoinette Sibley; and Anthony Dowell whose Enzo Plazzotto sculptures adorn my home. When I left Star I made sure to secure an agreement to carry on using the box at The Royal Opera House. This, of course, ended when the company was subsequently broken-up.

Peter Hall agreed to back me all the way and I set up a new company called LMG Film Productions. An early Multi Vista film recorded one of Antoinette and Anthony's performances at the Royal Opera House. Peter also collaborated with us to film a version of *Miss Julie*, starring a young Helen Mirren.

Multi Vista wasn't perfect, but it opened up so many possibilities. One of the biggest challenges was the technology wasn't yet quite advanced enough to be able to capture very fast movement. It was not a problem for actors, but if dancers moved too quickly, the video would appear to show multiple limbs on the same shot! We did, however, manage to edit the pilots sufficiently to get a reasonable quality of recording.

I was feeling optimistic about the way LMG was going when, out of the blue, I received a call from the National Association of Theatrical and Kine Employees (NATKE), the union which acted for theatrical, stage and cinema employees.

'We want you to stop video filming theatre productions,' announced their representative, quite curtly, over the phone.

'I beg your pardon?' I said, a little taken aback. 'Is there some problem?'

'Well, yes there is,' the caller said. Then he paused. 'We are concerned that your Multi Vista productions are to the detriment of our members.'

'But how?'

The man sighed, as though this was a ridiculous question.

'You are not using our members,' he said.

'This is an additional business,' I said. 'It does not encroach upon the normal studio work and will keep the talents of performers on record for the future. Indeed, we might even be creating *more* jobs, because if this takes off we'll be able to make more videos and maintain historic records of important stage performances, which in turn will employ more of your technical members. We would all win.'

'We don't see if that way,' he said blankly. 'We've had a discussion about it among the union executive and we want you to stop.'

I couldn't believe they'd had a debate about this and I hadn't been given the opportunity to put our case forward. The union seemed to have no understanding whatsoever about what we were trying to do.

'I'm not sure you have the authority to tell me to stop filming,' I said at last, sounding defiant.

'That is an interesting viewpoint,' he answered slowly. 'I should perhaps remind you that the projectionists in your Classic chain are all members ...'

His voice trailed off.

'Are you threatening me?' I exploded. 'Are you saying my projectionists will walk out if we continue to use Multi Vista?'

'It is not a threat,' he said calmly. 'Just a suggestion of what might happen. Who am I to predict the future?'

It was a threat though. We both knew it. The ground-breaking Multi Vista project was dead in the water before it had really got off the ground. If I dared to plough on regardless I risked destroying my burgeoning Classic and Essoldo cinema chain. I had no choice. I had to abandon Multi Vista and my dreams of producing a catalogue of films celebrating the finest performers of our generation.

This wasn't the only time I was faced with the power and intransigence of unions. Peter Hall and I kept in close touch after we began working together on Multi Vista. Indeed, while I was living with Linda Thorson and he was married to another actress, Leslie Caron, the four of us used to spend time together. Very often, Peter and I would bemoan the lot of an actor's other half, who were often left behind while their partner was off touring or filming.

Peter became director of the National Theatre and was deeply involved with the final construction of the three theatres we know today, which dominate the imposing building on the South Bank. He asked me to come along and take a look, knowing I had extensive experience in the field. When I looked at the site, I was quite confused. It seemed that so many back-stage elements in each performance venue were being replicated. An electrician who might be working in the Olivier Theatre would not have access to the Lyttelton Theatre, and technical crew in the Dorfman, renamed The Cottesloe, would not be able to use the back stage facilities of the Olivier. It didn't make sense.

'There is nothing we can do about it,' Peter said with a resigned shrug, when I pointed this out. 'The unions won't allow it.'

'Why don't you simply say; if you don't accept it, we won't be able to afford to open the theatres at all?' I pressed. 'They'll have to work with you then, or they will lose out completely.'

Peter wasn't willing to play hardball with the unions though and the situation still abides today. In my view it is a waste of hundreds of thousands of pounds every year, which would be better spent on the productions – or a reduction in the enormous tax payers' subsidy.

CHAPTER NINE

My negative experience with Multi Vista didn't manage to put me off my passion for the performing arts. Indeed, I felt as strongly as ever about theatre and cinema, despite my somewhat mixed experience so far. When Ray Cooney, my erstwhile partner in LMG, came to talk to me about starting a joint venture in theatre, I was ready to listen.

Ray had also been talking to the actor Brian Rix because the pair went back a long way. Brian had achieved considerable success in the West End, most notably for the Whitehall farces of the 1950s and 60s, and had produced about 90 theatrical transfers to TV, which is a record unlikely to be ever achieved again.

Ray and Brian had a common interest, in that they were concerned about the decay of some of London's best-known theatre venues. Although they felt passionate about reinvigorating the ageing infrastructure of the arts, they also knew they were a little out of their depth. While they were the best at their art in front of the spotlight, they knew little about the business of building and renovating theatres. That was where I came in.

The business idea under discussion was a plan to take over and refurbish certain theatres and then, once they were ready, to re-open them with productions to recoup some of the cost. I was enthusiastic when we met-up to kick around some ideas, but I did have reservations.

'Tell me about it,' agreed Ray. 'Half the battle is persuading a show to come to your venue and then, when they do and it turns out to be a stinker, they want a rent reduction.'

'Which leaves the theatre the choice between going dark while they start the whole process again, or losing money,' I broke in. 'It is certainly easier in cinema. You know what you are dealing with and the films only have a short run anyhow. It leaves the cinema management plenty of time to concentrate on other things like selling popcorn, chocolates or ice-cream. Incidentally, what do you think the penetration of ice-cream would be in theatres?' I asked both Ray and Brian earnestly. 'Perhaps we should be thinking about recouping more of our costs that way.'

I'd barely finished saying this before I was surprised to be interrupted by gales of laughter from the pair.

'Penetration of ice cream?' Brian chortled. 'Are you having a laugh?'

'We weren't thinking of putting on *those* sorts of productions,' chimed in Ray through fits of giggles.

I guess we come from different worlds. My commercial language might have sounded amusing, but I was making a valid point. If we were going to take a serious position in London theatre, we had to make money. I was, however, fully committed to restoring venues that had been poorly maintained for years, and that meant I had to accept a certain amount of risk.

I did have some recent first-hand experience of how a good venue, coupled with a successful production, can really make or break a theatre. A few years before getting together with Ray and Brian, I was approached by the producer Michael White. He had just completed the second week of a four week run of a new musical called *Rocky Horror Show.* It was at the Royal Court Theatre Upstairs, with the lead played by Tim Curry, who was unknown until then. It was also a first for Richard O'Brien who wrote the script, lyrics and music. Michael was desperate to find it a new home to extend the run in the Chelsea area.

Michael White made me a very attractive co-producer offer, which I could not refuse. He was clearly counting on the continuing interest of the audience to see the show. He did have a point, but while the audience response had been amazing, it had only been in a 60 seat theatre! I agreed to convert the Classic Cinema in Kings Road, despite the fact it was totally unsuitable for a live performance show like this because there was no stage, or a backstage. The show had to be re-written to fit into its new home and I employed a team of builders who were prepared to work day and night for the two weeks while the show completed its run at The Royal Court.

Amid some exciting publicity, the Rocky Horror Show transferred as to its new venue at the 230-seat Chelsea Classic Cinema, between August and November 1973. The show was so successful that I decided to agree to a further transfer to my new Cinema acquisition, also in Chelsea, the Essoldo. We had sufficient time for its conversion and in November of that year it won the Evening Standard Award for best musical. The *Rocky Horror Show* went from strength to strength after that. It stayed in its Kings

Road home for six more years, before moving on to the Comedy Theatre. My daughter Mandy became somewhat of a Rocky Horror Groupie, and she went to see the show in my theatre every week for about a year. She even paid for her ticket. She was not the only committed fan. The show was subsequently made into a film and the theatrical version is still playing somewhere in the world to this day.

In 1977, Ray and I had formed the Cooney Marsh company and Brian took on the job of Theatre Controller. The plan was that I would oversee and manage the revival of the venues, and Brian would subsequently place the productions in the theatres and take over responsibility for their management, dealing with licences, negotiating contracts and working with ticket agencies. At that time Brian was no longer enjoying eight performances per week and was very keen to take up a back-of-house role.

We set up offices at the Duke of York's Theatre in St Martin's Lane, but soon moved to larger premises overlooking Trafalgar Square. I brought in the first two projects, the Regent, near Broadcasting House in Regent Street, and the Broadway in Kilburn. Ray quickly added The Duke of York's and Ambassadors to our portfolio. These early projects gave us an indication of just how difficult the task ahead was going to be.

The Regent Theatre started life as a theatre and then became the Regent Cameo-Poly Cinema. By the time we got involved, it had been closed as a live theatre for the best part of 40-years and the backstage was in a terrible state of repair. Classic had been showing a season of

French language films but that market had dried up so the auditorium also required restoration, and to be upgraded as well for cinema theatre use. The polytechnic quickly approved the revisions since they didn't have the money to revamp the theatre. We hoped to recoup our costs with a successful run of shows.

The Regent had a "shoebox" shape with a small stage accessed from the equally tiny dressing rooms by a spiral staircase. We had to practically re-build the whole thing to get it into a presentable shape. Even so, once it was ready, it was a tough sell for Brian to get any production through the doors, and the ones that did usually only did so because they had virtually nowhere else to go.

The first of these no hopers was a production called *Little Willie Junior's Resurrection,* which had been described as a 'dramatic new musical experience' arriving from the States. It was, as everyone including the critics said, utterly cringe-worthy and quickly earned itself a rather ruder title in the offices of Cooney Marsh.

After a succession of other flops, we agreed to show Harold Fielding's rather risqué sex revue, *Let My People Come*. This turned out to be rather a good deal for both parties. Fielding was on the brink of going broke after a series of flops and we needed a decent run of a production. *Let My People Come* ran for 18-months and did very well indeed. However, as Brian rather ruefully pointed out, it had a specific market and that ran out.

'Once the dirty mac brigade and the tourists have had their fill, we'll be back to square one,' he correctly predicted.

For a while Brian speculated that the theatre had

some sort of curse over it. Most show producers certainly did seem to shy away from it. It was more a case of the theatre being too small for commercial productions than any sort of curse, but the fact remained that poor Brian had to actively search for anyone who might consider putting their production on in our venue. Takers were thin on the ground and a number of productions came and went, including *The Club,* starring my great friend Linda Thorson; *The Great American Backstage Musical*, with Marti Webb and Brian Protheroe; and *Sexual Perversity in Chicago*. Everyone in the Cooney Marsh office was hopeful about a Stephen Berkoff production called *East*, but sadly, that too went West very quickly. Poor Brian was tearing his hair out. It took a huge amount of effort to get the productions in and then, when the box office takings collapsed, he would have to encourage them with a reduction in the "nut". But all was to little effect.

Eventually enough was enough. I decided the best thing for it would be to convert the venue back to a cinema, and persuaded the landlords at Regent Street Polytechnic to agree to this change. They raised no objections and we immediately began screening the hugely popular film *Gone with the Wind*, which produced some decent box office receipts for about a year.

With two years left to run on the lease, the Poly informed us it would not be renewing our agreement.

'The students need the space to run their meetings,' I was told.

'But I have spent tens of thousands on the renovations and need to recoup.'

I knew for a fact these student meetings were only held about four times a year. It transpired that The Poly intended to carry out an even more elaborate, major revamp and the cinema was taking up important space which could become a major profit centre.

The Broadway theatre in Kilburn was chalk and cheese compared to the Regent. It was a decent-sized venue with a large stage and had adequate backstage facilities. It was a medium term leasehold venue – part of the Essoldo chain that I bought in 1972 – but was in such a state of disrepair that it had closed in 1973 and had been unused ever since. In earlier years, the venue had been through a range of uses and monikers, from Kilburn Vaudeville to Kilburn Empire, and I believed it would do well if it reverted to its original use as a theatre. I employed Dowton & Hurst, architects whom I had used many times for cinema and theatre conversions. It was decided to refurbish the stage and dressing room areas to bring them up to modern day standards, and to sandwich a new auditorium between the circle and stalls of the old one to make it a more appropriate live theatre venue.

Brian, who was once again tasked with filling the refurbished theatre, pointed out the very obvious snag about the venue: it was in Kilburn High Road. People in the immediate catchment were not traditionally committed theatre-goers. These reservations notwithstanding, we managed to secure one form of regular income from the Broadway fairly quickly. A company called Shiv Films made a blanket booking for every Sunday to show Indian movies back-to-back from dawn until dusk. They didn't need, or want, any involvement from us and were happy to simply pay the rent. They were the perfect client: polite, always paid on time and no trouble at all.

Our first theatrical production was the *Aba Daba Music Hall* variety season which seemed to do OK, but was never going to run and run. The next show was also an initial success. Brian persuaded the producers of a show called *Flowers* to transfer to The Broadway. Starring the then hugely popular dance and mime artist Lindsay Kemp, *Flowers* had been a runaway success when it opened at the Roundhouse in Camden. Brian had, quite cleverly, figured one venue off the beaten track was as good as another, and talked them into transferring. He was absolutely right and the crowds duly followed. Sadly, not for long though. Lindsay had agreed to take his talents to Australia and he and his company moved on. Once again, we'd been on the verge of something good, but not quite made it.

After that we experienced a frustrating succession of 'if only' and 'nearly' moments, where we almost secured big productions, but just lost out at the last minute. We nearly became the temporary home for the Mermaid Theatre, but the founder Sir Bernard Miles was discouraged from the idea by his backers. Then, Michael Croft was looking for a temporary home for the National Youth Theatre, after their usual venue the Shaw Theatre was found to contain asbestos. He too was turned down by his backers. Even the BBC came to take a look, considering Kilburn as a venue for late night chat shows such as Parkinson, but the broadcaster rapidly retreated when they got offered better terms at the Greenwood Theatre in Southwark. We were left with a succession of temporary shows and pantos, but just couldn't seem to get a regular paying tenant.

Brian, who had been spending weeks running around the West End and beyond in an attempt to fill Broadway, came to speak to me and Ray about his concerns.

'We've had an awful lot of 'if onlys' for the Broadway', he began. 'We just can't seem to get the big one though.'

'Is there any value in reverting to a cinema, as we did with the Regent?' Ray asked, turning to me.

Brian agreed to meet with the film bookers and, even though film wasn't really his area of expertise, he did pretty well. He managed to secure an entire season of Clint Eastwood films and, for a while, the venue's future was secured. Sadly, though, we were only putting off the inevitable. The Broadway closed its doors in 1981 and the building lay boarded-up and derelict until a decade later when it lived out its last few years before demolition as a Quaser Laser Tag games centre.

During this time, our interests weren't simply confined to the Capital, or even just the UK. Brian, Ray and I got involved with the Billy Rose Theatre in New York, which had lain empty for years. The eponymous owner had died a few years before and lengthy wrangles over his multi-million dollar legacy had nearly put paid to the theatre after it stayed empty for years. We bought it and set about restoring it in partnership with the Nederlander Group, an American-based consortium which already owned several theatres. It seemed like a wise thing to do because we needed management on the spot. We initially changed the name to Trafalgar, to link it to the London Theatreland and the fact our office was off Trafalgar Square, but it was renamed the Nederlander Theatre in 1980. It was undoubtedly one of our more successful ventures. We opened with *Who's Life Is It Anyway?* starring Tom Conti, who had starred in the original long run at The Savoy Theatre. We had to get special permission from Equity to take his first part across the Atlantic. The venue re-opened to good reviews and ticked along quite nicely.

If I was hoping for a similarly easy time back at our West End venues, I was in for a disappointment. Take the Duke of York's for example. The theatre had been bought by Peter Saunders in 1961, but Ray had engineered a deal that we would be responsible for running it. To begin with, that seemed like an easy ride. The ever popular stars Terry Scott and June Whitfield were starring in a long run of *Bedfull of Foreigners,* and the theatre was full night after night. Of course, as always happens, the pair eventually moved on. David Jason, who was just beginning to gain a following thanks to TV's *Only Fools and Horses*, took over from Terry, and seemed like a safe pair of hands. However, as any actor would say, it is not easy to step into another well-known performer's shoes and, sure enough, takings quickly slacked-off. Once again Brian and his faithful assistant Jo Benjamin had to hit the road to find a replacement. Three shows followed, *Hedda Gabler, Laburnum Grove* and *Half Life,* all with moderate success. Interestingly, thanks to me, or more correctly, my then girlfriend Linda Thorson, *Half Life* very nearly never made it to the Duke of York's at all, despite Brian's careful negotiations.

Brian had been in long-term negotiations with Peter Stevens, the then General Administrator of the National Theatre, in a bid to secure the transfer. They'd gone on for what felt like months. I'd seen them many times chatting intensely in the Cooney Marsh offices, along with Jules Boardman, who was responsible for the National's marketing. When, at long last they had an agreement, I suggested they joined me and Linda for a celebratory meal at the Ivy.

It was a pleasant enough evening. At one point Peter leaned across to speak to Jules – unfortunately, at this exact moment, Linda did the same, in her case to speak to me, because I was sitting opposite. To avoid any collision, Peter threw out his hand to steady himself. Sadly, this coincided with the arrival of the waiter, complete with a small Primus to flambé the next course. The hot Primus landed on Peter's hand, causing an instant reaction and the waiter, who was in a complete flap, grabbed Peters arm and plunged it elbow deep into a wine bucket filled with iced water. Peter's face was a picture of agony, sheer mortification and embarrassment as he sat with his shirt and jacket sleeve swilling around in the frozen water. After that we had an agonising wait of a few days before Peter was prepared to sign the contract, or was even capable of doing so.

Sadly, even though the contracts were eventually signed and *High Life*, along with its star Sir John Gielgud, duly transferred, our joy was short-lived. Sir John would only agree to a limited season and in a matter of four months we were back to hunting around for new talent once more.

My film production links with Tigon and Compton were also coincidently linked to my love of theatre restoration. Spike Milligan was keen to make a film about McGonagall, the Scottish poet who wanted to become poet laureate to Queen Victoria. He asked Joe McGrath, a Scot, to co-write the script for *The Great McGonagall* and also to direct the film. They found a location on the Thames where an old music hall called Wiltons was laying derelict following serious damage from the blitz in 1941. Indeed, the adjoining area was still a bombsite. The film was made in 1971, but to do so, the budget included a major restoration of the music hall so that it could be used as the main studio. The cost was supposed to be lower than hiring a studio, but in fact the restoration included replacing the roof and it went over budget.

Wilton's dressing rooms were used for the scene where McGonagall was locked up in jail when he arrived in London after his trek down from Scotland. Peter Sellers played the role of Queen Victoria. The film was a flop but the Wiltons Music Hall was saved and in 1972 received English Heritage Listing as Grade Two. Sir John Betjeman, who had tried to help me save the Queen of the South, used his influence to get the building listed, so at least we managed to save one valuable national asset together.

My involvement with the Shaftesbury Theatre was a far more uplifting experience on both a professional and personal level. The venue, which was built in 1911, came to my attention in July 1973. It had been home to the long-running musical *Hair*, when it came close to a disaster. A large chandelier had detached itself from the ceiling and crashed into the stalls just moments after the audience had vacated their seats at the end of the show. If it had happened just minutes earlier there would certainly have been many deaths. The chandelier was installed below a sliding roof partition which was regularly opened to 'air' the theatre. Decades of condensation and rain had eroded the fixings on the chandelier until it finally gave way.

In the months that followed, the future of the Shaftesbury looked very uncertain indeed. As well as needing an entire new roof, much of the stalls had been destroyed by the collapse. To begin with a property company took over the lease, but when that went bust the banks stepped in. Another property company took up the mantle and applied for permission to convert the Shaftesbury to an office block. The idea, quite understandably, horrified many in the theatrical community and a 'Save the Shaftesbury' campaign led by the actor's union Equity, secured some very high profile backers. Sir Alec Guinness himself picked up a placard proclaiming 'Over My Dead Body!' and won widespread support. When I came in with an offer to take over and refurbish the theatre, my deal was met with open arms. The building was placed on the Statutory List of Buildings of Special Architectural or Historic Interest and I pledged to restore it to its former glory.

Following the completion of the old Winter Garden Theatre in Drury Lane for EPC and its re-opening as The New London, this restoration of The Shaftesbury was my most ambitious West End theatre project and I had to use shares in my property company as collateral. The cost of the repairs was so cripplingly high, I had to call in as many favours as I could to achieve them. I even had to enlist my father to help, putting his excellent building and plumbing skills to good use. I still have a vision of him, even now, perched high up on some scaffolding with a tin of gold paint, touching-up the cupids on the boxes.

The theatre re-opened with *West Side Story,* but by far the most successful run was *They're Playing Our Song*, staring Tom Conti and Gemma Craven, which opened in October 1980 and secured Gemma a Laurence Olivier award. In between those two productions we had a series of dreadful flops. One of the most awful by a long way was *Le Grand Magic Circus* by the French Argentinian theatre director and actor Jerome Savary. I went along to the first night and could tell straight away it was a stinker. Still, we went through the usual routine and duly rounded the evening off with the obligatory First Night Party.

I had a heavy heart when I followed the cast and crew to the Chelsea Rendevous restaurant in Knightsbridge. I think everyone knew this production was going to be pretty short-lived, but were trying to make the best of things. I was with one of my then girlfriends, sat around a large round table of ten, when a rather pretty brunette opposite me caught my eye. What was most noticeable about her was her delicate hands were both balled into tight fists as they rested on the table's surface, and the top of her knuckles were quite white. She was clearly very tense and not at all happy to be there.

All of a sudden, she caught me staring at her and looked a little alarmed. I smiled and pointedly balled my fists up tightly and then slowly opened them and waggled my fingers as though loosening them up. Her face relaxed and she smiled. She'd got the message and slowly unfurled her fingers and gave them a little waggle too. I nodded in approval.

I felt a little frustrated. I was too far away to speak to this lovely woman, even though I very much wanted to. All I could do was listen in to snippets of conversation as she spoke to the tall man beside her. I knew him quite well, which is why he had tickets for the first night. He was a Scot called Gordon Provan, a director of one of the divisions of Rank Technical with whom I had placed some significant business over the years. From what I could pick up from my eavesdropping, this young lady worked in publishing for MacMillan and was apparently editing a children's encyclopaedia.

Brains as well as beauty, I thought approvingly, resolving that I would find a way to speak to this lady come what may. It was not to be though. Sadly, before I could open a conversation with her, Gordon whisked his companion away.

The following day I called MacMillan Books. I had managed to find out the mystery woman's name was Gillian and asked the receptionist to put me through to 'Gillian in the children's encyclopaedia department'.

When she picked up the phone I knew straight away I had the right Gillian.

'Oh, hello,' I began. 'It's Laurie Marsh. We almost met last night. You didn't look like you enjoyed the show much.'

'The man with the knuckles,' she laughed.

'Yes, that's me. Are your hands feeling better now? I was getting worried about you.'

She laughed again. She had a nice laugh and seemed much more relaxed now.

'Listen, I wanted to get in touch to ask if you'd like to come out with me?' I said. 'How are you fixed tomorrow night?'

'I'm playing bridge, I'm afraid,' she said.

'How about the night after that?' I pressed.

'I'm really sorry, but I have plans for the evening too,' she answered.

Was she trying to give me the brush off, or is she genuinely busy, I wondered? There was only one way to find out.

'OK, what about a night next week?'

'Alright,' she said. 'I can do that.'

I could have punched the air. I was already totally smitten by this girl. I hardly knew her and couldn't explain it, but there was something about her that I really liked. Over the next few weeks and months those feelings only grew deeper as I got to know Gillian. This woman was truly my soul mate. We had many parallels in our lives and, as a result, understood each other entirely. Like me, Gillian was an only child and came from a home where her parents seemed rather indifferent to her opinions. In her case, her father was busy running his company (which made airplanes in Northern Ireland where Gillian was born). Her mother had been quite ill with a drink problem from which she fortunately recovered and has been in good shape ever since. At the time of writing she is now in her 96th year. Over the years Gillian had become fiercely independent. After getting a good degree from Trinity in Dublin she had come back to England and become involved in publishing.

Gillian was every bit as intelligent as I suspected on that first night and I began to often seek her counsel. She certainly proved consistently wise over the next of Cooney Marsh's big renovation projects, the London Astoria in Charing Cross Road. I acquired the Astoria from Rank in 1977. It was being used as a cinema and I re-designed the interior, converting it back to theatrical use. Among the many jobs we undertook was to raise the stalls by five feet, and we also changed the lighting positions to better frame the stage. I was really pleased with the result and spent a long time with Ray and Brian discussing which show we would bring in to kick off this remarkable new London theatre experience. The first production was *Elvis the Musical,* staring PJ Proby. It opened on 28 November 1977 and won the Evening Standard's 'Musical of the year Award' the following year.

Elvis the Musical had all the signs of being our most successful venture to date. The audiences loved it and for a while it looked like it would run and run. Unfortunately, we had a very big problem: PJ Proby had been a stand in for the real Elvis on various shows in the USA. He didn't look much like the star until the make-up artists had worked their magic, but his voice sounded almost exactly like Elvis's. It was uncanny and the audiences adored him. Sadly, though, PJ Proby was not the most reliable performer. He was invariably late for each performance and in the end we had to organise a minder to make sure he got to the theatre on time. The pressure was really on because strict Equity rules required that all performers were at the theatre *at least* half-an-hour before the curtain went up. The final straw came when the actor got into a rage and destroyed the apartment we'd rented for him in Wigmore Street. He caused thousands of pounds of damage and we couldn't let the situation continue. We let him go and hired another actor. We should have held a national competition to find the new Elvis as sadly, the show didn't do half so well without its popular star and Ray became keen to shelve it and try something else. I argued and argued in favour of carrying on with *Elvis the Musical*. I was convinced it would pick up but I got nowhere. That was the unfortunate part about my relationship with my Cooney Marsh colleagues: I was not the artistic director. My job was to get the theatres together, fund the renovations and then, if there was any money left over, I would use the asset of the building to fund the shows. I felt rather vindicated after the subsequent show, a stage production of *Grease* staring Tracy Ullman and Sue Pollard, flopped after a brief three-month run. This was followed by the equally unsuccessful show *Beatlemania*, which was very much championed by Ray. He was convinced the audiences would come flocking to see our Beatles tribute show. They didn't. In 1980, *Ipi Tombi* transferred from the Cambridge Theatre, but once again the run was limited and it closed after four months.

The next musical to grace the Astoria was *Yakety Yak*, which opened in January 1983, but only lasted a few months before being replaced by *Jukebox,* a 'musical extravaganza' featuring songs of the Fifties, Sixties and Seventies. To be fair, *Jukebox* was fairly popular and filled seats most months, however, it ran out of steam by the end of the year.

One of the last theatrical shows at the Astoria was *The Hired Man,* based upon the book by Melvin Bragg (who I got to know very well) and produced by Andrew Lloyd Webber. The music was the first full theatre production by Howard Goodall who is now one of the best-known composers in the UK. *The Hired Man* should have been a box office winner, it certainly had all of the correct ingredients, but it opened in the same week that Mrs Thatcher decided to save The Falklands. The TV coverage of the war was too much for us. In a bid to save the show I agreed with Melvyn and Andrew that we would forgo our charges, and the cast all agreed to work for equity minimum. This move should have enabled the show to survive the war. Maybe it would have done, but we never got to find out. After a short time, Andrew 'put up the notice' without our agreement and the show closed. The next show was *Lennon*, which also failed to enthral audiences and simply added to our mounting losses.

After this series of flops it was obvious a re-think was needed. Casting around for ideas, I decided to transform the Astoria into London's first-ever dinner theatre. My idea was, in part, inspired by Bernard Delfont, the Russian-born theatrical impresario. I had recently become friendly with Bernard, along with his brothers Lew and Leslie Grade.

Bernard, or Bernie as I knew him, had undertaken the hugely successful conversion of the London Hippodrome into the Talk of the Town nightclub. It was attracting a large number of top-name performers such as Frank Sinatra, Shirley Bassey, Eartha Kitt and Judy Garland. I wanted to do something similar with the Astoria and spent a lot of time talking to Bernie about how to make a go of it.

'You've got to be able to hold on to it for three years and keep changing the show,' he advised. 'The aim is to get tour groups booking ahead with you, like they do with the Mousetrap.'

I listened carefully to what he said and brought in architects Dowton & Hurst, along with a team of trusted builders from my cinema business, to undertake the conversion. They enlarged the steps of the balcony to create a wider and deeper tier to enable seating and tables to accommodate up to 400 diners. Kitchens and serveries were constructed at the back of the auditorium for self-service. We also added a retractable cinema screen so films could be shown before shows.

When it re-opened as a dinner theatre, with a transfer of *Wild Wild Women* from The Orange Tree Theatre in Richmond, it did reasonably well. Indeed, it launched the West End careers of several of the artists, but it was always a bit of a struggle. One of the final straws came when bar staff stole two weeks' worth of takings. This was one of the few areas which did make any cash. I had had enough and ditched the dinner theatre idea. The Astoria was converted into a live music venue by removing the seats in the stalls, adding a bar to the rear stalls and converting the circle to nightclub-style seating with tables. The Astoria began attracting pop groups of the day and the basement Ballroom became a gay nightclub called *Bang*. But these new incarnations also attracted the wrong sort of crowd. The venue quickly gained a reputation as the 'go to' destination for drugs. We had to have bouncers on the door and an almost permanent police presence inside.

'You really don't want to be associated with that sort of thing,' Gillian wisely advised. 'The sex and horror flicks maybe, but owning a famous drugs centre is not for you.'

She was absolutely right, I didn't want a reputation as a Soho Drug Lord, so I put it on the market. I sold the lease for £1 million and made a reasonable profit, even taking into account the two conversion costs and the losses from shows. In 2008 the news came through that the once famous theatre was to be demolished to make way for

The Astoria eventually closed its doors in 2009, and was demolished as part of the Crossrail development

the new Crossrail station in Tottenham Court Road. The Astoria closed its doors for good in January 2009 after a farewell concert aptly called the 'Demolition Ball'.

During these events, Cooney Marsh had amassed some serious debts and the situation was becoming critical. By the time I sold the Astoria, Brian was already out of the day-to-day running of the business, even though he was still officially a director. He hadn't agreed with some of the shows that Ray fancied for some time. He and Ray were always chalk and cheese in character and Brian, who had a cautious nature, was uncomfortable with some of the risks Ray was taking. When, in 1980, an opportunity came up to chair the charity Mencap, an organisation close to Brian's heart, I agreed to release him immediately.

What Brian didn't realise was he could still be liable for a significant share of the £610,000 of debts (equivalent to over £2.5 million today) we had amassed with Lloyds Bank. If he had, it would have terrified him. He would almost certainly have lost his house if the loans and overdrafts were called in and we were nearing that eventuality. It was a pretty terrifying prospect for Ray and me too, so it was time to act. We sold our half-share of the Nederlander Theatre in New York to our wonderful partner there, Jimmy Nederlander for $850,000 (£348,000) and I took over the remaining bank debts myself in exchange for retaining Cooney Marsh interest in the Shaftesbury and Astoria. By doing this and selling all the assets of Cooney Marsh we were able to settle the debts.

Ironically, some years later, Brian did end up facing loses of £1 million plus, but for completely different reasons. Following an operation to fit a replacement valve in his heart, he became very anxious about his wife Elspet. He hated the thought that if she outlived him she'd fall into any sort of financial difficulty and arranged for her to become a Name in a Lloyds syndicate. The worst possible thing happened and it lost a tremendous amount of money. There is, of course, unlimited liability as a Lloyds name and Elspet's share of the debt was just under £1 million. Poor Brian. Here was one of the most famous men in British theatre, a knight and a lord, and a tireless campaigner for charity – and he faced losing everything at the age of 80.

With my very good friend, The Lord Rix of Whitehall

Brian and Eppie had sold their home in Barnes and moved to a new home in Wimbledon. He obtained an equity release on the house and persuaded banks to give him a generous loan. After extensive negotiations, Lloyds took a reduced sum so at least that was dealt with, but the pair still faced tremendous debt in their dotage. I couldn't bear it and resolved to do what I could to help them.

'You have to let me do something,' I said to my good friend. 'I have a plan. Leave it with me.'

After a huge amount of effort and negotiation, I managed to obtain planning permission to build on the site of their Wimbledon home. The existing house was not particularly attractive but it was in a great location on a private road. I envisaged a large new modern residence with a swimming pool in the basement and a tennis court in the grounds. After putting it on the market with fully drawn-up and illustrated plans, I managed to secure a deal for almost £2,700,000 by negotiating with several would-be purchasers at the same time. The purchaser had made some delaying conditions to the high purchase price. He wanted to go one stage further and build two residences and agreed to pay a substantial monthly fee as a deposit while he explored the options with planners. This process went on for some time, as it always does, so by the time the deal was finalised, Brian and Elspet secured a tidy sum from both the land sale and the monthly fee. They were able to buy a house outright in Esher (which was close to their daughter Louisa), pay off their bank debts which had by then risen to £1.3 million, and have a secure sum left over to guarantee them a comfortable retirement.

I was happy to help Brian and Elspet who were always among my most cherished friends. While the end of Cooney Marsh was the close of another chapter in my life, but it didn't end my love of theatre, or my involvement with either Brian or Ray who remained close friends. The one irony in this story was that after all the failed productions and the seemingly endless search for the winning show, Ray went on to write and produce just that shortly after we parted company. *Run for your wife* ran in the West End for nine years, spanning theatres from the Shaftesbury to the Aldwych, and eventually was made into film. That's the luck of the draw in this business. It takes just one show to change everything.

This was not my final brush with the theatre business though. In 1982, Edwin (Ed) Mirvish decided to buy the Old Vic Theatre in London's Waterloo. He was a very successful businessman and philanthropist in Toronto, Canada, where he owned several very large warehouse, retail and restaurant businesses, with an extraordinary reputation for giving customers best possible value that earned him the nick-name 'Honest Ed'.

Ed was very keen on theatre and restored The Royal Alexandra in Toronto in 1963, as well as funding the Princess of Wales Theatre in 1993. Ed introduced me to his son David in 1982 and I subsequently spent some time assisting him with the restoration of the Old Vic, on which he lavished $4 million. The Old Vic won a number of national awards during the Mirvish ownership, which continued until 1998 – indeed more than any other theatre in Britain.

David continued with the tradition and paid for the restoration of the Pantages Theatre in Toronto. It was renamed Mirvish Theatre in 2011, to honour Ed who died four years earlier.

I didn't completely leave the theatre business myself either. When Cooney Marsh broke up, two of my managers, David Cole and Guy Kitchen, came to see me and said they wanted to carry on with theatre work. They wanted me to head-up a new company which would manage theatre productions and suggested that it would be my name over the door. I said I would arrange funding for them and act as chairman, but they were better off creating their own identity and leaving my name out of it. They agreed and made quite a good living for around 20 years.

As for me, well, let's just say Gillian and I received about 40 pairs of free tickets. We were happy with that though. I've never lost the enjoyment from a night at the theatre and still enjoy it today.

I preferred saving theatres, not acting in them!

CHAPTER TEN

In my career there have been some spectacular successes and some equally spectacular failures. I'd see an opportunity, do the maths and go for it. It wouldn't always work out, but when it did, the returns reflected the level of risk I was prepared to take, which is why in the rollercoaster ride that was my career there were some very big ups and many very big downs.

The disappointments hurt, of course they did, but I never ever let them get me down. This was in great part down to three people who had an enormous influence on my thinking.

The first of the three is the Maltese physician and inventor Edward de Bono. Edward was the originator of the term lateral thinking. I read his books on the subject many times and they taught me how to think in a completely different way. I honed his technique of looking at a problem from the outside. It is very easy to get immersed in your troubles, so much so it is almost impossible to see a solution. It is far better to float above or beside them, to view them for what they really are from a number of different angles. I've always found this impartial way of looking at things helps me come up with solutions that are always so blatantly simple once I've seized upon them that I (and those I share them with) wonder why it has never been thought of before.

•••

The second major influence is more personal. It was Harold Furst, senior Vice President of Bank of America. I first met him on my honeymoon with my first wife Liz in January 1962. Liz and I were staying at The St Francis in San Francisco.

Financially, things were a lot different back then. There were no cash machines for ready access to your cash. Additionally, there was a curious rule in place where it was illegal to take any more than the equivalent of £50 in cash out of the UK. I'd done everything I could to get around this rule, even making an application to the Bank of England itself saying I needed a larger amount for 'commercial reasons'. It was a logical enough argument – I already had some business interests in the US by that time. They weren't having any of it though. The powers-that-be were convinced it was for personal, not commercial, reasons and I couldn't really deny the fact that I was on my honeymoon.

Inevitably, I ran out of cash just a few days into our trip. Ironically, my situation coincided with a business meeting with a contact called Gerson Bakar, who had coincidently employed my secretary/PA Suzanne Castle, who had left to move to America. Gerson was a very successful developer. His company had rebuilt the whole of the San Francisco water front.

'I have a bit of an immediate problem,' I told him, after we'd chatted about a few projects. 'I am short of a few dollars. Actually, to be specific, I am short of any dollars at all. This crazy £50 rule has really been a pain.'

'Let me introduce you to my bank manager Harold.'

'Harold?'

'Yes, Harold Furst at Bank of America, he's quite an incredible guy. You'll love him. He's head of economics there and has an amazing story.'

'Go on.'

'I don't know it all, but basically he had to support himself as a kid after his parents died. He pretty much did anything and everything to put himself through university, renting deck chairs and all sorts. He had a real entrepreneurial zeal. By the time he was 19-years-old, he was already teaching at Berkeley, while he was doing his PhD. He founded the banking economics department which went on to turn out some of the most effective bankers – they in turn enabled the Bank of America to become the most successful bank in the world at that time. Pretty impressive, eh?'

'He does sound it,' I agreed. I already sensed I'd like to meet Harold. It would be very informative and I was really looking forward to speaking with him.

In a matter of hours, I was being introduced to Harold Furst at Bank of America by Mr Bakar, who helpfully gave his friend a potted history of our own association.

'How can I help you,' Harold said, after he shook me warmly by the hand and we'd gone through the usual getting-to-know-you pleasantries.

'Well, I have rather fallen foul of the £50 rule,' I said. 'I need to get some more money, but unfortunately I can't pay the bank back.'

'No problem,' he smiled. 'How much do you need?'

'100 dollars,' I said.

Harold leaned over his desk, picked up a slip of paper and scribbled something on it.

'If you go to that desk over there they will give you $100,' he said, handing me the slip.

I did so and as soon as I had the cash went back to thank him.

'This is wonderful Harold, but isn't this is the bank's money?' I said, slightly anxiously.

Harold laughed. He seemed quite relaxed.

'Listen Laurie, I have never lost money for this bank and I am not going to lose it with you,' he said. 'When you can pay it back, you pay it back. You're a friend of Mr Bakar, so I won't even charge you interest. In fact, it's almost lunchtime, come across the road and I will buy you lunch. You won't have to crack into your $100.'

By 4pm when the bank closed we were still there, chatting away like old friends. He told me how he had been persuaded to leave Berkeley to create an economics post at Bank of America because they were really concerned that he would pass on his vast knowledge to all of their competitors. He agreed to join them as a senior head office VP for a pre-agreed contract on his own terms.

From that day on until the day he died, we remained close friends. We met up every year, initially with Liz and then later with Gillian. He had split with his wife, but brought his delightful partner Alice with him to stay with me at Podenhale. We went on tours of The Silk Route in Turkey, The Paradores in Spain and the Rainforest in Australia. Together we travelled down the Danube from

Vienna to Budapest and spent time also in Prague whilst the Russians were still there. (We returned a couple of years later after the Russians had moved out and saw the enormous changes that democracy had achieved in such a short time.) We flew over to San Diego for his son's wedding and then we drove right across the USA. Harold and Alice also spent some time with us in London and in Lunas at our twelve-and-a-half-hectare estate there. We kept in constant touch by letter and phone and often talked about life – and occasionally even about business. I loved his 'can do' attitude. In Harold's mind, anything was possible and he would never let the slightest set-back push him off course.

My third source of inspiration was Buckminster Fuller, the American neo-futuristic architect, systems theorist, inventor and author, who I always viewed as the least understood and most influential genius since Einstein. He developed numerous architectural designs, the most famous of which was the geodesic dome, which saw thousands of his domes pop up all over the world. He was the sort of man who when told something couldn't be done, he would do it anyway. I saw him on a lecture tour in England and was inspired when he told how he invented a 'Dymaxion' – a car that could park sideways – and then built it. That was in the 1930s, when vehicle technology was in its infancy. He also invented a pre-fabricated, energy efficient Dymaxion home which didn't require any services and, again, defied the naysayers by simply going ahead and building it. He refused to set limits on what could be done simply because it had never been tried before. I was so inspired by his approach I went to every lecture he gave in the UK and often thought about his philosophy when I was presented with a seemingly insurmountable problem.

I needed to draw upon the skills I had learned from all three of these men when I did business with Lew Grade in 1979 and came close to losing everything.

I'd been friendly with the Winogradsky and Delfont families, which contained Lew and his two brothers Leslie and Bernie, for years. The family was steeped in showbiz. Lew and Lesley Grade started out their careers jazz dancing when they were very young. They went on to became theatrical agents and Lew, in particular, made a big name for himself. Bernie, who was less charismatic and really quite shy, went his own way, but still did very well for himself, rising to become chief executive of EMI, which owned the ABC cinema chain.

My first real business association with the family, other than Bernie's input on the Astoria, was when Lew asked me if I would help him resolve a serious problem on a film called Capricorn One. He had not been able to obtain a West End venue for the premiere. I came up with a novel idea of offering him the use of two venues on the same night: one at our major cinema in Haymarket and the second location at the multiplex in Oxford Street. The release of Capricorn One was a success and Lew and his wife cut the tape for the re-opening of the Haymarket Classic.

He subsequently decided that he would like to incorporate a chain of cinemas into his entertainment conglomerate, Associated Communications Corporation. Lew asked me to meet him at his office in Great Cumberland Place, whereupon he proposed a take-over bid for my group. However, to ensure that the deal was a success, he wanted me to negotiate a 51% acceptance of the bid before it was made public. I did so, the offer was eventually made, and I joined the board of ACC and ITC their film production subsidiary.

The tape cutting for the UK premier of the film 'Capricorn One' at The Classic Centre in Haymarket, with Lew & Kathleen Grade and Reg Dowdeswell

My agreement to have a closer association with Lew was primarily prompted by the project I was working on opposite the Windmill Theatre. The scheme had been rumbling on for nearly a decade whilst I assembled this large site and bought out the tenants. I was in grave need of a cash injection. ACC owned the Stoll Moss Theatre Group and it seemed a natural extension for them to have this large, new theatre at Piccadilly linked to a very large building programme. Lew's offer was either shares, or a mixture of cash and shares, amounting to a total of £13.5 million for the whole group of companies. I thought that I had a long term future in ACC, so I took shares. The deal included my cinema chain, the Bingo Clubs leased to Mecca, my UK and International property interests through the Laurie Marsh Group, which included The Airport Park Hotel in Los Angeles.

Unfortunately, I wasn't immediately endeared with my co-directors because the Daily Telegraph wrote a piece proclaiming me as Lew's heir apparent. Lew himself assumed I had planted the story with a view to taking control of his company, but it just wasn't true. All we had discussed was that I would become a director and that ACC would enable me to continue to expand my group within the parent company because I had some large scale plans. Doing the deal with Lew was really a choice between borrowing the money for expansion, or joining a conglomerate and using their credit. The idea of me succeeding him had never been discussed and I had not considered the eventuality, but the newspaper article really put the cat among the pigeons.

There was a major disagreement with Lew after he thought that I wanted his job, and when the deal was found to include a large overseas share purchase there were suspicions that all was not how it should be. I felt I was in the clear because, although I had made some minor purchases to enable me to deliver the 51% Lew had demanded, I had no Swiss Bank account, nor did I buy shares there. Executives from the stock exchange called me in to answer questions about the overseas buyer and even hinted that this was me. Later it emerged that Stephen Kornis, one of my co-directors, had bought a number of shares. After he died, his executors found that he had bought these shares in Switzerland where he had retained the proceeds.

This subsequent discovery came 45-years too late to help me. In the ensuing row, I was asked to resign and paid a very large compensation of £125,000. At the same time, it transpired that ACC was in serious financial trouble, which might have gone a long way to explain the haste to get me out of the door. All of my assets were sold off within a few weeks in a desperate bid to save ACC. That was undoubtedly one of the main reasons for my pay off and removal, which was linked to a tough agreement of confidentiality. At least the severance deal hadn't included my theatre interests with Cooney Marsh, so I had some show-biz links to keep me busy. And I also still owned a small family property company. I had sold a large number of the shares before they went through the floor and used the money to buy myself and Gillian a family home in St John's Wood. I also bought an amazing lower penthouse

The deal with Lew Grade received a significant amount of media coverage

in Key Biscayne in Florida for my parents, fulfilling a promise I had made 15 years earlier to them. Finally, a large town house in Turtle Bay, New York for my children.

This is a good point to digress for a moment. My father had invited me to see him and my mother one evening.

'This is for you,' he said, handing me a cheque.

I looked at the figure on it. It was for £50,000.

'What's this all about?' I asked.

'As you know, the shops are sold, the house has been sold, and that is most of the after-tax balance. It is all we have except a few thousand in the bank. From today, we want you to look after us.'

This seemed fair enough. My parents had certainly

gone above and beyond, scrimping and saving to send me to Perse School. It couldn't have been easy, but it had given me a fantastic start in life. I certainly had no doubt a great deal of my success was down to my schooling, although I have to admit that I did obtain some leadership experience whilst I was in the army during my compulsory conscription. I left with the rank of lieutenant and was upgraded to captain during the reserve period of five years, which was also compulsory.

When we had this conversation in late 1965, my father was 63-years old and my mother was 57. How was I to

SARAH and DAVE
1927

Saturday 31st January 1987

MENU

Cocktails - Lancon Black Label Champagne
Joseph Perrier et Fils Champagne Magnums

* * * * *

Hors D'oeuvres & Canapés

* * * * *

Salmon Écosse Frais Poché - Sauce Mayonnaise
Les Salades Variés
Chablis Premier Cru 1985 - Côte de Lechet

* * * * *

Boeuf en Croute avec Sauce Madère
Vegetables du Saison avec les Pommes
Nuits St. Georges - Chateau de Premeaux 1982

* * * * *

Roulade de Chocolate
Salade des Fruits du Saison Frais
Bombe Glacé

* * * * *

Armagnac VSOP   Le Café   Brandy VSOP

* * * * *

Music by
Ronnie Carroll & The Doug Perry Trio

MABEL and ALBERT
1937

A Diamond Wedding Anniversary for my mother and father, who were married in the same week (but ten years before) as aunt Mabel and uncle Albert. This was therefore a 110th wedding anniversary and the menu was the same one that they had enjoyed 60 years earlier.

know my mother would live to 100! Joking aside, I made sure they lived a life of luxury, sharing their time equally between the penthouse in Florida each winter and the flat in St John's Wood. I know that they were happy with the way things turned out.

To digress still further, during the trip to purchase the penthouse in Florida, I had flown over with Gillian by Concorde to impress her, and it did. We then flew up to New York where I wanted to really impress her again with 'Chapter Two'. The story is quite simple. I knew Neil Simon from whom we had obtained the rights to put on the very successful '*They're Playing Our Song*' at the Shaftesbury. The great score was written by Marvin Hamlisch. Neil wrote some wonderful comedies, many of which had been filmed. One of his plays, called *Chapter Two*, had been at The Lyric in Hammersmith, where the female lead had been played by Gillian's cousin Linda Bellingham, the amazing actress who died so tragically in October 2014. The 1979 film version of *Chapter Two* was also a favourite of ours. Neil Simon's autobiographical story related to the death of his first wife and his reluctance to pursue a new relationship – hence *Chapter Two*. James Caan played the lead and Marsha Mason, who happened to be Neil's wife at the time, played his girlfriend and the film was centred around a magnificent NY town house. I said that after our trip to Florida to buy the apartment for my parents, we would fly up to New York and I would buy us a town-house ... our Chapter Two. We found an advert in the Times classified that Sunday and agreed to buy a house in the famous Turtle Bay there and then in January 1980. The house was large and it had seven flats, many with tenants. I registered the purchase company in the name of my three children. There was a great deal of complicated restoration work to follow and time spent moving tenants out, but eventually it became a valuable source of income for over 30 years. I sold it for the children in January 2014. Unfortunately, the company ended up with a $1.5 million tax liability which wasn't particularly pleasant, but of course it was directly related to a very handsome capital profit. The way to reduce the tax would have been to sell the company but, after several months, the agents said that it was not going to be practical because the deal was too small. Too small! Would you believe it?

Now, back to my brief stint at ACC. I feel I should explain more about the financial troubles that were clearly closely connected with my hasty departure. Not only are they key to the direction my life took, but provide valuable insights for any business person.

Lew had committed everything to make a film called *Raise the Titanic* based on the Clive Cussler book of the same name. It had a budget of £18 million, which was a small fortune in 1978, and Lew told us at my first board meeting that he had pre-sold it to Fox in the United States, all rights to the USA and Canada in all media. What didn't emerge then was that somewhere deep within the small print was a line that said something along the lines of: if Fox didn't like the quality of the rough cut (and importantly the term 'quality' was not defined) they could reject the film and the contract would be null and void.

In perhaps a taste of things to come, the film began haemorrhaging money almost immediately. Lew repeatedly rejected the pre-production models of the Titanic and it seemed impossible to get the script quite right. Up to seventeen writers came and went as Lew's team struggled to get the story into a saleable state. When the mock-up of the Titanic was finally completed, the 10 tonne, 50ft scale model was found to be too big for any existing water tank. The production crew (and Lew) had a big decision on their hands; reduce the size of the boat, or increase the size of the tank. The minimum cost they faced to do either was $7 million and both options would seriously delay filming, thus further driving the film into the red. They plumped for increasing the size of the tank and, in fact, ended up building a whole new horizon tank at the Mediterranean Film Studios in Kalkara, Malta. The writing was, however, already on the wall for *Raise the Titanic*, which like its namesake was destined to sink – in this case without a trace. Fox hated the rough cut when they did eventually see it, they invoked the get-out clause in their contract and after that the film really struggled. It eventually grossed just $13.8 million against a budget expenditure of over $40 million.

Although Lew quipped publicly that it would have been cheaper to 'lower the Atlantic', the failure of *Raise the Titanic* was a complete disaster for him and sent ACC spiralling into debt. Faced with imminent financial catastrophe, he took the easiest available option open to him and began selling assets at a tremendous rate. And what assets were all neatly valued, packaged and ready to sell? All my companies of course, which had only recently been signed over to ACC

Everything I had worked so hard to build was sold off as quickly as possible. My chain of cinemas, Town Markets, and my UK and International property companies were all put on the market and quickly snapped up. Town Markets included around 750 small shops within large stores, giving opportunities for small traders to get on to the best-selling locations such as Carnaby Street, Kings Road Chelsea, Knightsbridge, and Kensington High Street. It was nothing short of a fire sale. Many of the deals were at utterly the wrong time in the business cycle of the individual assets.

Take a hotel I had acquired in Los Angeles, for example. Stanley Margolis, the finance director of my group, had first brought the idea to me five years earlier. He was running things for one of my companies over in the States at the time.

'I know some people here in LA who built a large hotel and conference centre adjacent to the racetrack and they have been ripped off. They granted a management contract to Hyatt who used this new hotel for transferring bookings to fill up their own one nearer to the airport and they have got themselves in a mess which they would love to sort out,' he said. 'I told them about your interest in hotels in the UK and they are interested in selling to us'.

I had a certain amount of experience in hotels at the

time, so I certainly wasn't going to dismiss the idea out of hand. I'd built and converted hotels in the UK and for The Rank Organisation in Albufeira, Portugal and had a seat on the board of a large London hotel group called Centre Hotels, after Star bought a large share in the company a few years back. The deal was in partnership with Maxwell Joseph of Grand Metropolitan Hotel Group, which also owned Mecca and I had a close working relationship with its CEO Eric Morley. Stanley said the US race-track owning group wanted $4 million for the Airport Park Hotel with nearly 400 bedrooms and shared car parking for 30,000 cars, mainly for the race track of course.

My main difficulty in trying to do this deal was I didn't actually have anywhere near the sum of money in question. As always though, I thought laterally and looked for ways around this barrier. I asked Stanley to set up a meeting with the representatives of the American group who owned the Airport Park Hotel. I asked Henry Edwards, the CEO of Centre Hotels, to manage this LA hotel for us. He was a very efficient hotelier with vast experience. We agreed some reasonable terms for the management and Henry introduced a couple of really good executives from one of Centre Hotels' top hotels in London who would move to LA and take control if I was able to negotiate a deal.

I flew to LA to meet up with the racetrack owners early in 1976. One of the directors was an elderly lady who was keen to avoid litigation with the Hyatt Hotel Group, but did not want to see if they would get out until they had an acceptable alternative owner in place. After some

*The very profitable Airport Park Hotel, that was sadly sold off
by Lew Grade*

interesting negotiating, she and her co-directors proved keen to do a deal. They agreed to accept a down payment of 10% and to give my company a mortgage over ten years at a very low interest rate of 4 %. This required us to pay out only $144,000 interest for the first year and, after that, we would repay both capital and interest.

We were half way through paying off this mortgage and the hotel profits were going through the roof when Lew stepped in and pulled the plug, selling off the Airport Park Hotel at a good deal more than he paid us and Stanley and Henry were out of a job.

It was heart-breaking seeing this hotel and all my other businesses sold off in quick succession, one after the other. I couldn't do anything but watch because I no longer had any day-to-day involvement and I couldn't even complain, or try to put my side of the story, because I had signed a legally binding confidentially agreement which gagged me completely. Worse still, the successful group of businesses that I had built up and had wanted to expand was now gone.

It was ironic really. The reason I went in with Lew was to fund my business investments, but he ended up losing both my businesses and his own defunct company. This true story has never been made public until now. There was no point being bitter though. I had cashed in the majority of the shares after paying tax into family assets and although that was not the original intention, it has turned out to have been quite a good outcome all these years later. From a practical, business point of view, I had no choice but to pick myself up and start again. I had done it before after my brush with King many years before. Now I would do it again.

CHAPTER ELEVEN

I didn't have long to wait before a very intriguing business project came my way via Stephen Weeks, a film director, novelist and playwright I had known for some years. When we first met he was just 20-years-old and he knocked on my door to ask me to invest in a film he wanted to make. He'd left his home in Wales and been up and down Wardour Street in his quest to get funding for a movie about World War One. Everyone had turned him down flat, perhaps because *1917* was a short 30-minute film and no one could see the point of investing in shorts. But the earnest young man intrigued me. In another example of my occasional bouts of inexplicable Marsh madness, I chose to back him. I was impressed by the rough-cut pilot I had seen and believed he had talent. My faith was subsequently rewarded when *1917* won a Silver Bear award in Berlin.

Stephen and I kept in touch over the years, although we didn't make any further films together. I was aware he had bought a very small castle in Penhow, near Newport, in South Wales and was busy trying to restore it.

'You must come and see it,' he urged.

I did not get around to it for a long while, but following the Lew Grade episode I decided to take him up on the offer. Gillian and I dropped in to see him on the way to visit family in Cardiff.

He was the same old Stephen, brimming over with ideas and full of enthusiasm. He'd built a film studio in the ramshackle barn across the road from his castle and was full of grand plans. It was another, smaller project he mentioned that intrigued me though. He had started a company called Soundalive Tours and was using Sony Walkmans, then a very new technology, to provide audio commentary for tours of his castle. People would pop in a pair of earphones, switch on the cassette player in their pocket and be treated to a professionally produced guide. I thought the idea was inspired.

'I thought you'd like it,' Stephen said. 'Can you imagine how this could take off? We could get them in every stately home and National Trust property in Britain and that's just the start.'

Typical Stephen, he'd already assumed I'd be right on board and would invest in his new venture. It was clear he did have something though.

'OK,' I said. 'I'll back this.'

'Fantastic, I've got some great ideas. We definitely need to target the States too. They'll be all over this and we need to get in fast...'

When I returned to London, I put the wheels in motion to back the business and fund the expansion Stephen had outlined. I mentioned the idea to Brian Rix, who had recently stepped down from his role as Secretary General of Mencap (he became emeritus President), and he immediately saw the potential, particularly how it could be used to help the disabled. He joined Soundalive Tours too and also suggested that Admiral Sir John Cox, who had recently resigned from the Spastics Society, might also be an asset to the board. They were both valuable additions to the venture and rapidly opened up many doors. Brian's son Jonathan also became involved, writing scripts for tours with particular emphasis on helping the disabled enjoy the experience. Another high profile presence on the board was Sir Roy Strong, the former director of the National Portrait Gallery and the Victoria and Albert Museum.

It may not look it, but this was cutting edge technology!

The biggest problem we had with Soundalive was investment. Not only did we have to buy hundreds of Walkmans, but technology was advancing at a dizzying pace. It was almost impossible to keep up and to do so we needed very deep pockets. Everyone was so inspired by the concept that they were all willing to chip in, but what we didn't realise was it was beginning to create a real problem for us internally. While I put in a fair bit of money, as did Brian, Sir John and various other investor friends (including John Hawkings-Byass of Spanish wine fame), Stephen did not have access to capital. He became more and more resentful as he saw his share of the business diluted because people were being given an equity stake in return for their investment. We discussed it many times and I offered to loan him some cash to invest, but he turned it down flat, saying I should *give* him money.

In the end it all came to a head and Stephen and I had a huge row. Stephen's view was that Soundalive was his baby and we had trampled all over it. He had a point in that it was his idea, but the company would never ever have got off the ground without significant investment. It's impossible to operate in a market that relies on technology if you are not prepared to keep pace with the latest gadgets. We had repeated rows about it and Sir Roy Strong actually left the venture, saying he couldn't possibly be involved with such a volatile character as Stephen. Sadly, we couldn't work out an amicable solution with Stephen, so Brian, John and I had to end our involvement in Soundalive too and the company was eventually sold.

I never really managed to revive my relationship with

Stephen. I tried to one time, when Stephen had a row with Technicolor (which for a short time was owned by another good friend, Harry Saltzman) over the colour development of one of his films. I used all my contacts to intervene and raised the dispute to the highest level, which had Technicolor executives running around for months trying to investigate the problem. However, when it was proved incontrovertibly that the issue had nothing to do with Technicolor and was most likely caused during filming, it was probably the final straw for our already fractured relationship. Stephen now works and lives in Prague. He has written a couple of heritage books and is restoring castles there.

My experience with Soundalive did have one positive result. It helped me formulate an idea that had been in my mind for a while. I decided I wanted to become more involved in the charitable sector and certainly wanted my future work to have a philanthropic edge.

Throughout the highs and lows of my business career I never forgot the promise I made to Keith Barry. I said that if ever I became a millionaire I would make a sizeable donation to Perse School and I meant it.

I'd stayed in constant touch with Keith ever since I had left Perse and he was still a huge influence on my life. If I ever needed advice, I would often turn to him. I tried to see him as often as I could too and particularly whenever I had a new car: Keith still loved cars very much. Mind you, on one occasion I came a little unstuck.

A couple of years earlier, around 1967, I had bought

a handmade car called a Peerless, which was being manufactured in Bromley, Kent. The Peerless was a good looking, sleek sports car, with its bodywork constructed from formed fibre-glass. On the way with Liz to see Keith and Beryl in Cambridge, I had to brake very sharply and somehow the seat became disconnected from the chassis. I had to get a rope and find a way to bind it all together to complete my journey. Then, to pile on the ignominy, the driver's door turned out to be completely jammed when I eventually arrived at Keith's house. Keith couldn't stop laughing after he saw me wind down the window and crawl out of it!

I managed to recover some face when, a few years later, I joined with some friends to secure the UK distribution rights for a new hand-built sports car, the Monteverdi. We had been obliged to order a dozen of the very beautiful, but rare, Swiss-brand sports cars but it was well worth it. I drove one to Keith's house to show it off because I knew he, above all people, would appreciate its design. It went some way to helping me overcome the earlier embarrassment.

This was, sadly, not to be the end of my run of comical incidents with malfunctioning cars. In 1973, I bought a yellow V8 Aston Martin to impress my guests at Podenhale. I subsequently lent it to my board colleague, Stephen Kornis, because by then I had the Rolls. After a year or so, Stephen found it a bit too fast and parked it in the driveway of his new house in Victoria Road, Kensington, just behind Cumberland House. From time to time I asked Stephen to let me have the Aston back but it never seemed to happen. It wasn't until he became quite ill in 2013 that he asked his secretary to give the keys back to me. Sadly, the car's locks were so corroded due to years of neglect, I had to get a garage to break a side window to drag it away. It was a clear sign I should avoid buying flashy cars in the future!

A stunning hand-built Monteverdi

I was 35-years old when I became a paper millionaire thanks to my various property investments and business ventures. One of my first priorities was to phone Keith.

'Keith, I have done it, I am a paper millionaire,' I announced to him over the phone.

'A *paper* millionaire?' he said, pronouncing the word 'paper' slowly.

'Yes, I don't actually have £1 million in the bank, but my various assets are now worth in excess of that figure,' I explained, even though I knew he was perfectly well versed in the notion of a paper fortune. 'I want to make good on my promise. I want to make a donation to Perse.'

'That is good news,' he said, sounding genuinely pleased. 'Congratulations and thank you so much.'

Keith had just started fundraising for Perse, so this proposal meant a lot to him. When I said the sum I had in mind was £30,000 he was completely bowled over.

'It would seem you are the second property developer to have a substantial impact on the school,' Keith said, referring to Stephen Perse who founded the school in 1615 with a donation valued at £10,000 – an enormous sum at that time.

I rather liked that thought. It was nice to know I was continuing a tradition and it felt even better that I was furthering it at a place I held in such high regard.

The money was used to build a sixth form centre which opened in 1970, and my donation was celebrated by a plaque on the wall. I have continued to make regular significant contributions to the school to increase the bursary fund and the number of students that can be admitted to Perse on merit not money.

It wasn't until 1980, when my main business changed so completely thanks to my experience with Lew Grade, that I began to consider taking on a wider range of philanthropic work. Once I started to think about it, I began to question why I hadn't done more in the past, even though I knew the answer was that I was working flat out on my various business interests. I couldn't help but reflect on my time at Star, where I had grown deeply uncomfortable with the largesse of my fellow directors. In fact, Rothschild's Bank, who had a representative on our vast board of directors, set up a charitable trust for me into which I donated most of my dividends. All that my co-directors seemed to be concerned about was where the next bonus was coming from so they could buy yet more possessions they didn't really need. My discomfort at this attitude ran very deeply inside me and probably always has done. Now I was no longer involved in the daily cut and thrust of the property and entertainments business, I had more time to do something positive about the inequalities that had frustrated me for so long.

Interestingly, one of the first and significant philanthropic projects to come to my attention was one which combined my desire to help other people with the core skills I had been developing within the theatre industry. Jeremy Fry was an inventor, engineer and entrepreneur who founded the Rotork Engineering Company. This was where a young James Dyson was employed as an engineer and designer before striking out on his own. James Dyson came to see me after he left Rotork. He had designed a unique new bag-free vacuum cleaner. He asked me to invest £250,000 for a large equity share. I was involved with Soundalive and Libertas, so I turned him down.

What a mistake that was!

Jeremy Fry had built his company to become the market leader in oil and gas pipelines and highly specialized pumps. Fry had a keen interest in the arts and, in 1979, bought the Theatre Royal. At that time the theatre was in desperate need of renovation. By coincidence, Fry spotted an article about me in an architectural magazine, which discussed my work on the Astoria and Kilburn Empire theatres, as well as the construction of The New London Theatre in Drury Lane. Endeavours like this were unusual; although a handful of theatrical groups were profiting very handsomely from their productions, no other company was concerning itself with renovating the UK's aging theatre network. This fact didn't escape Fry.

'I understand you've been restoring theatres,' he began, when he and some of his colleagues came to see me in my office at my house in St John's Wood. 'Our theatre has been neglected for nearly 100-years and we don't have anything like enough money to do anything about it. How would you feel about coming to Bath to help us?'

I was flattered to be asked, but had a number of reservations. The first was purely practical: Bath was well over an hour-and-a-half away by road, and in those days the M4 motorway had not been constructed. The rail links were dreadful too. Secondly, the deal being discussed here was nothing like the usual way I worked, where I bought the venue, funded the restorations and then tried to recoup my costs via subsequent (hopefully sell-out) shows. This was purely a philanthropic venture where I would employ my specialist knowledge and experience and walk away at the end of it. It would involve an entirely different way of thinking and fundraising for a project like this would be very difficult. No regular funding sources were prepared to invest in theatres. It would be an enormous struggle to get anywhere. I was keen to get involved in charitable projects, but I wasn't yet convinced this was the best one for me.

'What's your budget?' I asked.

'We have had estimates of between £3 and £4 million' Jeremy replied.

'How much do you think you can raise?'

He paused and took a deep breath.

'Well, we've got a number of local dignitaries who are prepared to put up some cash. Everyone feels very strongly about keeping the theatre going.'

I waited for him to go on.

'Over a period of time for fundraising we expect to raise up to £50,000, possibly a bit more'

'Is there any money available elsewhere?' I pressed.

'Well, the city wants to save the theatre. It is the only one we have. There is support at borough and county level too. I've spoken to them all and believe we could probably raise as much as £400,000 from the various local governments if it is spread over a couple of years. I've also spoken to the Arts Council and they've said if the locals put up £400,000, they'll match it.'

So, they had offers of just over £800,000 against a budget of £3 to £4 million. The disparity in the numbers was so huge.

'You do realise this kind of project never ends up

costing 'just £3 or £4 million', don't you?' I said.

Jeremy laughed.

'I was hoping that with your input and experience that we could do it for less,' he smiled. He seemed to think this was genuinely possible.

'It will go the other way, it always does,' I said.

Once we had talked it through in more detail, I ended the meeting by saying I would give it some thought, but deep down I really wasn't sure. The Theatre Royal in Bath seemed like such a big project and they were so far off from raising the sum they needed.

Our hands were forced just a few weeks later. The proscenium arch, which framed the stage, parted company with the main building and the council promptly condemned the theatre. The more the building inspectors investigated, the worse things became. It emerged that the foundations had all but gone, the basement was flooded and the three large underground brick vaults were plagued with rats.

Jeremy Fry called me once again.

'We have to try to persuade you,' he said. He sounded desperate. 'Bath is a very important tourist city and it only has this one theatre, please say that you will help'

'OK, I'll come and see it,' I relented.

When I finally got to see the theatre I could see straight away why its backers were so passionate about it. The Theatre Royal in Bath is considered to be a prime example of Georgian architecture. It was just shy of 200-years old when I first saw it and had an impressive array of ornate plasterwork, and gilt and red decoration. It was easy to understand how, in its glory days, it had earned a reputation as one of the most important theatres outside London.

During my visit and in the days that followed, Jeremy and his team continued to press me to commit, offering me all sorts of incentives, ranging from an honorary degree from University of Bath, to (somewhat bizarrely) putting me up for a knighthood. They needn't have worried. I had already decided I wanted to help get this lovely venue back on its feet.

It took three years to finish the renovations and I used all the skills I had learned on my projects with the Shaftesbury, Astoria and Regent Street theatres, as well as ones honed in my property businesses. I converted the cavernous basement vaults into bar and restaurant facilities and opened up the brick arches to create new relaxation areas for theatre goers, locals and tourists. In addition to the major architectural refurbishments we put in new backstage facilities, structurally under-pinned the auditorium and fly tower, brought in all of the technical equipment for sound and stage, as well as replacing the house lighting which was totally out of date. I also instigated a deal to buy the Garrick's Head public house next door. I pulled so many strings to get things for cost, or even free, Jeremy and his team could scarcely believe it. Architect Donald Armstrong from Dowton & Hurst, whom I had been using for some years now, worked for expenses only, in return for my guarantee to him of work elsewhere. And chemicals giant ICI was even persuaded to provide paint for nothing. Where I couldn't get people to help out, I put my hand in my own pocket, funding (among other aspects of the build) the theatre seating and the number one dressing room.

The transformed Theatre Royal Bath re-opened in November 1982 with a gala performance of *Midsummer Night's Dream* attended by Princess Margaret. The Royal National Theatre Production starred Paul Scofield, Susan Fleetwood and Tony Haygarth and before the show the people behind the three-year project were introduced to the Princess. I was secretly rather pleased that she became so absorbed in chatting to me about what had been done and how we managed it that the start of the show was delayed. The lights had been dimmed, the large chandelier in the middle of the auditorium had been raised, the curtain was ready to be lifted and myself and the Princess were still talking! Jeremy had to come over and give me a tap on the shoulder.

'Can we let the Princess sit down, so we can start the show,' he said pointedly.

This was the highlight in my first philanthropic venture. Although I had never embarked on this scheme for recognition, I felt slightly irked that my role was almost ignored once I had done all I set out to do. My name is featured in a plaque in the Theatre Royal foyer celebrating contributors to the renovation, along with the names of thirty or forty others who also played a part. I also got my name on the number one dressing room, the refit I personally paid for. My honorary degree never transpired. Indeed, a year later I received a polite, yet short, letter from University of Bath saying they only gave a handful of these gongs out each year and they did not have one for me. I never even got a letter of thanks from Jeremy Fry or his team, even though I saved them many millions. The actual overall cost was around £5 million, which is the equivalent today of about £35 million. I stayed on as chairman of the development company for two years after completion of the project to ensure that the theatre had adequate cash-flow.

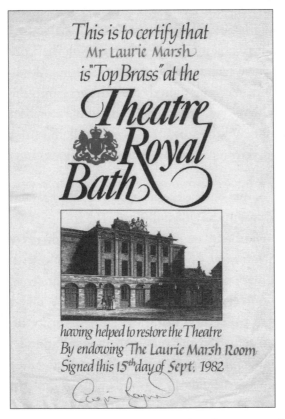

This is to certify that
Mr Laurie Marsh
is "Top Brass" at the

Theatre
Royal
Bath

having helped to restore the Theatre
By endowing The Laurie Marsh Room
Signed this 15th day of Sept. 1982

The enormous effort required to save the Theatre Royal Bath
was absolutely worth it

If I thought it was a hard slog dealing with campaign groups like the one steering the Theatre Royal project though, that experience paled into insignificance when dealing with local authorities. Although I had regularly come into contact with them while working on my commercial property projects (and often had to bite my tongue at their intransigence when it came to attempting to do what was clearly the right thing), I now found myself coming up against them time and again in my philanthropic work. Perhaps I was naive to imagine that doing something for the good of the community would get everyone supporting my efforts. As I quickly discovered, nothing could be further from the truth. If anything, working on charitable projects was more difficult because everyone and his dog seem determined to have their say and bring things crashing to a standstill.

One of my first experiences of this was when I got involved with the Roundhouse Theatre in Camden. I became chairman of a charity tasked with reviving the distinctive former railway engine shed in North London, working with such luminaries as Melvyn Bragg, my dear friend Brian Rix, and Glenda Jackson. We had a lot of innovative plans for raising the large quantity of money needed to refurbish the venue, including building a block of flats and some houses on a neighbouring site. One of the reasons for the delay was a dangerous skeleton in the cupboard. I had been made aware of an asbestos dump on the adjoining site where we wanted to build the flats. It had come into being when the railway engine dome had been converted into a theatre in 1964. The asbestos, which was used for fire protection, was removed and dumped on the adjoining land that was also owned by the London County Council (the precursor to the GLC). Ownership of the land transferred to Camden Council in 1983. No one wanted to make a big fuss about it, but it was made clear my budget had to include provision for the specialist removal of this 60 tonne asbestos dump.

Nothing we suggested ever seemed enough though. Camden Council met every idea we suggested with dithering and delays. It was hugely frustrating and the situation rumbled on for years – and all the while the venue suffered. After months of not really understanding what the problem could possibly be, it eventually emerged that the sticking point was that Camden Council wanted the Roundhouse to be specifically run by and used for ethnic minorities. The big problem Camden had with this aim was they didn't have the knowledge or wherewithal to find anyone sufficiently qualified or interested enough to take up this strategy.

We went backwards and forwards offering solution after solution yet nothing seemed to satisfy Camden Council. I had agreed to co-opt the productions from The Royal Exchange Theatre in Manchester, which was ideal because it had a similar configuration. The artistic director, Braham Murray, came to see me and we agreed to co-produce and give The Roundhouse an enormous artistic advantage. But, this was not enough to impress the intransigent local authority. The people that I was talking to had never heard of The Royal Exchange, nor did they appreciate the artistic advantage of the link I'd secured.

All the time this was going on, the building remained unused and with every passing week became more and more dilapidated. Eventually, in 1996, after more than a decade of lying empty, Camden floated plans to turn the venue into an architectural museum. This prompted local businessman and long-term Camden resident, Torquil Norman to buy it for £3 million. He managed to succeed where we failed, raising £7 million for the Roundhouse Trust. It re-opened in 2006 as a 1700-person performance space.

My experience with the Roundhouse was child's play compared to the one I had with Alexandra Palace. Alexandra Palace, or Ally Pally as it is more widely known, has a chequered history. Located between Muswell Hill and Wood Green in North London it had to be rebuilt just two years after it opened in 1873, after a terrible fire. It is probably best known as a home of the BBC, but has also served as a theatre, entertainment venue, horse racing track, and even an internment camp for German and Austrian civilians during World War Two. In 1980, after Haringey council took over Ally Pally from the Greater London Council and set about refurbishing it, the venue was once again almost destroyed by fire.

This is the point that I came in, when they offered a 125-year lease out to tender, with requirements to restore the whole building. When I first went to view the site I was quite shocked by the state it was in. At least half the buildings had been destroyed by fire. The outer walls were intact, but the interior was wrecked, the theatre had virtually gone and parts of Ally Pally's famous organ had disappeared. Brian, Ray Cooney and Eric Reynolds joined me on my initial visit because they were also keen to get involved in the restoration of such a prestigious venue. We all understood straight away that this was a substantial project, but we could see the potential.

Over the next few months I assembled an impressive consortium of around a dozen nationally recognised businesses, and in a remarkably short space of time managed to negotiate pre-lettings of all of the proposed new elements. I signed up a hotel company which was keen to take over the lease of a new boutique hotel; a cinema group which would lease a six screen multiplex; and a brewer to set up a real ale centre. I even made arrangements to restore the first TV studio in the world as a museum. I also secured a formal funding offer. My proposal was a who's who of leading names in any field you could imagine: Wembley Stadium, Allied Entertainments, Healy and Baker, Binder Hamlyn, Jones Lang Wooten and Berwyn Leighton were all on board. It was easily the most impressive consortium I had ever seen and I would go as far as to say one of the best teams assembled in history. Not only that, our joint proposal would have created over 1,400 jobs. Not surprisingly, I was rather pleased with what I had achieved.

My alarm bells should have rung when, during a public presentation at Alexandra Palace, a short while before the tenders were due, I was approached by a man closely connected with the project.

'What is it worth to you?' he said, somewhat bluntly.

I could hardly believe my ears. Was he asking me for a bribe? I was aware this sort of thing went on, but it certainly wasn't my way of doing business. I decided the best way to deal with this unorthodox approach was to simply walk away and I did.

Perhaps I shouldn't have been surprised when, a short while later, it was revealed my consortium hadn't won the tender. It was awarded to a group which claimed to have had a funding offer from my old friends at Grand Metropolitan Hotels. Intrigued, I called Maxwell Joseph, who confirmed to me that they had agreed to take a lease of two restaurants and the boutique hotel, but NOT to provide funding for the whole project. The tender had been won under false promises. My team and I were hugely disappointed and so were the members of our blue chip consortium which had worked so hard.

Then (and this was perhaps even more galling), after Haringey instructed their legal department to grant the wining team a 125-year lease, it emerged that the local council didn't actually have the legal right to grant the lease at all! The entire tender process had been run on a false premise. I was utterly furious. The team had put so much time and money into this project and yet the opportunity had never really existed. Worse still, Ally Pally remained a crumbling hulk, with no sign of any work being done.

After that, things went from bad to worse. As both

Brian and Ray reflected, the ensuing story was worthy of becoming one of the farces they used to write and perform in. It gradually emerged that one of the key people had recently been made bankrupt. The project stumbled from one crisis to another as Haringey councillors attempted to recover the situation, yet every step they took just seemed to make things worse. One of their first solutions was to grant the winner of the tender a temporary lease; but, perhaps predictably, given what had gone on so far, that didn't work out too well. Eventually, Haringey was forced to buy them out and start the whole process again three years later.

I thought about tendering again and even looked at the terms briefly, but I was so fed-up with the whole thing that I decided to steer clear. History proved me correct. The council managed to run-up a £30 million deficit. Haringey was subsequently heavily criticised in an official report into the funding and the attorney general ruled the overspend was unlawful. The council refused to accept this ruling and claimed it was, in fact, 'owed' £30 million by the charity overseeing the work, even going so far as to charge compound interest on the debt. Eventually, with the arrears at £60 million, Haringey decided to recoup the losses by putting Ally Pally up for sale. As of now, the venue has still not been sold and still continues to lose the borough of Haringey millions of pounds each year. Haringey announced in January 2015 that they were going to spend about £30 to £40 million to restore the TV Museum and the theatre. It beggars belief that so much money has been wasted, particularly when my original proposal was at no cost to the tax payer whatsoever.

That development was, however, by no means the only frustrating not-for-profit venture I became involved in. I was once invited to a meeting with London Zoo and asked for suggestions on how to raise money. I suggested that they made use of the car park close to the Wolfson Centre. Parking could be taken underground and the existing space could be used for two or three Regency Style large houses, which would sell like hot cakes in that location. I got a little way down the line with this plan, having drawn up designs and floated the idea to the Royal Parks, who seemed to be in broad approval. Then, the site was visited by Prime Minister Margaret Thatcher who made a point of shaking my hand and thanking me. Less than a week later, the Treasury handed over a cheque for £2 million. She wanted good publicity for the forthcoming election and had clearly decided supporting the zoo was a vote winner.

Often, when I first become involved in a project, it is hard to predict which way it will go. This was certainly the case with two more theatre projects: LAMDA and Core Arts. The outcome for each couldn't have been more different.

I was invited onto the finance and general purposes executive committee of LAMDA in 1977, by one of its most successful alumni Brian Cox, who was a close friend of mine. I was elected chairman of the Trust in 1992. It had been painfully obvious for years LAMDA didn't have nearly enough room in its Kensington Mews Theatre site and I decided I would use my time as chair to address this. I devised a project to extend LAMDA's theatre and build a dedicated costume area, which was something the drama school never had. The project involved working with a church which was immediately behind the main building, the aim being to make use of some of the chancery. In addition, some of the space beside the existing theatre would be used to create six new homes, which would finance the rest of the project. The entire scheme relied on the full cooperation of the local vicar who had complete control over the church. I was hopeful he would be on board and there was every indication that this would be the case: he already had close links with LAMDA and the church hall was regularly used for overspill classes.

However, at the eleventh hour, after a number of property consultants had put in a lot of on spec work to the project, the vicar had a falling out with some people at the Academy and pulled the plug on the whole project. If that wasn't galling enough, one of the architect partners demanded payment, despite the fact everyone had agreed to a deal where they would only receive fees if and when consent was granted. This particular man denied all knowledge of such an agreement citing (rather conveniently) that if there had been an agreement it had been made with a senior partner who had since passed away. By contrast, the quantity surveyors who had also been present with me at all of our meetings confirmed that there was no question of a charge in the circumstances. This intervention cost LAMDA £20,000 and they had nothing to show for it because the project never went ahead.

I couldn't help but remember this experience when two architect friends asked me if I could help with a project for the charity Core Arts in Hackney. Core Arts promotes artistic and creative activities for people with severe and enduring mental health issues. Once again the scheme would involve working closely with a local church because Core Arts wanted to build a new arts facility using the church hall and the vicar's house. I came up with a design for a new hall in the church garden and went to speak to the local vicar, fearing the worst after my experience at LAMDA.

'Oh, we don't need all this,' said the vicar when I explained all the perks and incentives we were offering for the land.

This vicar had not long been in the job and in his view his predecessor had asked for concessions that weren't really needed. He concluded: 'Why don't we just give you the hall? It needs massive restoration. You do that and you can let us use it now and again. We'll only need it for about ten days a year.'

That's exactly what we did and the whole thing went completely smoothly. I even managed to get planning permission to convert a couple of garages in the corner of the plot into flats, which I then gave to the charity. I could hardly believe it had all been so straight forward. It was entirely similar to the aims of the LAMDA project, but had a completely different outcome. If only all charitable projects were like Core Arts. But, as I was to discover with my next major scheme, some things just can't be done, despite the very best of intentions. Having a great idea which will save the tax payer millions is no guarantee of success.

CHAPTER TWELVE

The proposed redevelopment of the Royal National Orthopaedic Hospital (RNOH) in Stanmore, Middlesex gave me more sleepless nights than any other undertaking in my career. If I ever thought working with local authorities could be frustrating, working with government was a whole new ball game. In fact, it was a complete eye-opener that has forced me to reconsider my entire view of the world.

I was first asked to look at the RNOH by John Adams, a lifelong friend who had been receiving treatment there for cancer of his left hand and wrist. The RNOH provides the most comprehensive range of neuro-musculoskeletal health care in the UK, treating spinal injuries, complex bone tumours and providing rehabilitation for chronic back pain. It's a major teaching centre too and around 20% of orthopaedic surgeons used to receive their training there.

John had been under the care of Professor Tim Briggs, the senior consultant at RNOH and a Board Trustee, for several years. During the course of his treatment in 2011, Tim told John that the hospital, which had been founded in 1944 with the installation of temporary buildings to treat veterans from the 1939–45 war, was now falling apart. A large number of the sheds were vacant and the remainder were not fit for purpose. A major rebuild was essential but the Trust did not have the money. During his treatment John asked Tim to speak to me and Tim literally picked up his phone and called me whilst John was still in the treatment room. John arranged for us to meet and Tim subsequently asked me to have dinner with him. We met up at a Greek restaurant in Notting Hill and I agreed to see what I could do.

After conducting an extensive site survey, I proposed an innovative way to re-build the hospital on this sprawling 112-acre site, and turn the RNOH into one of the world's top hospitals with cutting edge medical services *at no cost to the taxpayer*. At a time when the NHS is virtually on its knees and still facing further cutbacks, you'd think the government and local authorities would have welcomed a positive project that came in at zero cost to the tax payer. But no, apparently a Public Finance Initiative (PFI) costing £260 million was an easier pill to swallow.

Let me go back a step and explain. The idea I came up with was relatively simple to describe and understand, but far from simple to implement. I didn't want the NHS Trust to sell their land to developers who would wring every little bit of value out of it and keep every penny for themselves. The site belonged to the NHS and by retaining the land the Trust would get the maximum benefit from it. My idea was for an alternative to the unbelievably costly Private Finance Initiative (PFI), which had already been put forward by the time I became involved. The Board of the Trust should transfer excess land on the site to their own fund-raising charity that was permitted to trade. I would then carry out the large scale residential development on this land. I arranged to get a top team together and to provide a viability study without charge. A Charitable Finance Initiative (CFI) would build the new hospital, a multi-storey car park, nurses' homes and all of the ancillary buildings in phases, as I simultaneously sold off the housing at a considerable, tax free profit which would go back to the Trust.

As mentioned earlier, I had already successfully used a similar method to fund the Theatre Royal in Bath. It provided a tax efficient way for the RNOH to use its assets and retain all the developmental value.

The executives of the Board of Trust were very keen when I initially presented it to them, but added that there was an important local pressure group called The Stanmore Society who needed to be brought on board to support my proposals – and of course the local planning authority needed to be convinced too. Over the next few weeks I completed some fine-tuning of the details of the project in preparation for presenting to them both. A glossy brochure was produced, illustrating just what could be achieved.

The Trust arranged a meeting at The Town Hall where Councillors had assembled together with several officers from the planning department. They gave us a lunch and then I presented my offer. They were whole-heartedly in favour, which was really encouraging. Next, I was joined by a representative from the Trust and the medical architects for presentation to the assembled numbers of The Stanmore Society.

'It's too good to be true,' was the first response I received.

This was not the first time I had received such a reaction to my development proposals. I assured the group of around 60 interested parties it was, indeed, true.

'Even if it is true, can you do it?' was the second question from the audience.

'I can,' I assured them. 'I just need your full support.'

'But the NHS is not in the property business,' came a familiar repost from the floor.

I have heard this one many times too, particularly since I began charitable work, and I am now ready for it.

'Every venture you can think of has to have some sort of land involvement,' I explained. 'I know that the Trust is not in the property business; they are in the business of providing a health service. I agree with that concept absolutely, no argument. You don't need to be in the 'property business' though. Leave that to people like me who are in the business of saving tax payers' money.'

Inexplicably, although most people at the meeting were eventually persuaded of the viability of my proposal, there was still one man who steadfastly favoured the alternative proposal: the PFI one. This was despite the fact the PFI was estimated to cost more than £260 million over the period of a lease, together with a parallel obligation to pass all repairs, maintenance and management through the landlord. These additional obligations were a normal requirement, but by my calculations could well cost another £150,000 during the 30-year lease term, bringing the total cost to the NHS in excess of £410 million. That's before you consider the fact that these large-scale projects inevitably require variations and amendments that cost additional money. I was convinced the PFI option could well reach £500 million. It later transpired that this single objector to my CFI proposal had been an ardent supporter of the PFI model at an earlier Stanmore Trust meeting. What I had to hang on to however, was that the overall response had been very favourable.

My next port of call was central government, and with the support of Lord Basil Feldman and his close friend Lord Norman Tebbit (Norman and his wife Margaret were still being treated by specialists at RNOH following the notorious Brighton hotel bombing in October 1984) I was hopeful we would make good progress. Basil and I go back a long way. We'd worked together right at the beginning of my career when I was making the Mickey Macs and we'd kept in touch ever since. I hadn't met the Tebbits before my involvement in the RNOH, but we got on well and I found their passionate support for my scheme a huge help.

After a great deal of lobbying, a meeting was secured with the then Secretary of State for Health, Andrew Lansley. I didn't waste a moment of the time I spent with him. I showed him the brochures, the list of companies I had on board and a funding offer from Barclays to the tune of £60 million. I emphasised again and again that this project would save the health service up to £500 million.

'This appears very impressive,' he said, nodding with approval. 'I would certainly like to look further into this.'

Of course, he didn't just press the green light. That's not how central government works. No, the Minister commissioned an independent review into CFI, by DTZ, an international valuation and surveying firm. I was at least hopeful we may be getting somewhere at last. My team was referred to NHS London, the group of civil servants based at Spire House at The Elephant & Castle charged with overseeing the health service. NHS London instructed DTZ, and my team were asked to supply a considerable amount of supporting data. The report was supposed to be delivered to the civil servants at Spire House and to our team within six weeks. I could barely contain my excitement. I felt sure that the outcome would be positive. There really was no downside to the proposal.

When the six week deadline came and went, I began to feel a little uneasy. Day after day went by and nothing transpired. Eventually, I decided to force the issue and contacted DTZ to find out what had happened.

'Oh, a first draft has been delivered to Spire House but we've been asked to make some amendments, hence the delay,' I was told.

Frustratingly, this happened again on two further occasions. We were given a deadline, which then got pushed back while Spire House requested changes. Something within the report was clearly not to the liking of NHS London.

Finally, late on a Friday afternoon in October 2012 the report arrived. With it came an accompanying letter from Peter Coates CBE, the NHS's Commercial Director with responsibility for oversight of the procurement of the PFI programme. It said bluntly that the report stated 'quite clearly' that it was 'not legal' to carry out the CFI scheme and the NHS 'could not and would not' take my CFI offer any further forward.

'We are not permitted to take the risk,' he wrote.

We were given until the following Monday to respond.

I was utterly gobsmacked and reached for the report to go through it in detail. My medical architect and Savills Survey team studied it line-by-line over the weekend. Our disbelief at the apparent conclusions quickly turned to anger when we studied what the report *really* said. While it stated that it would be illegal for the RNOH Trust to take on the role of speculative developer and builder, it had failed to acknowledge that this was not what we offered at all. In all the CFI documentation, we had made it clear that the charity would operate the CFI via a trading subsidiary. A charity operating a trading subsidiary is not an unusual arrangement. Indeed, of the 130,000 plus charities currently operating in the UK, nearly all have a trading subsidiary, even if it is only to sell Christmas cards. There was no reason whatsoever the RNOH couldn't have used their existing charitable trading subsidiary. It would have been the charitable equivalent of a PFI, except rather than the PFI taking all the cash, it would phase in profits from residential sales and start by building the first phase of the new hospital after infrastructure works. I had even arranged for the master plan to re-use most of the internal roads for the new development. My anger became even more intense when I came to the part where DTZ recommended that our scheme 'be allowed to evolve'. Nowhere did it say it should be rejected out of hand. Indeed, the only point it flagged was that if we failed in the endeavour, there would be an estimated loss of £20 million. Of course, this potential financial penalty paled into comparison to the £260 million plus cost of the PFI.

1O DOWNING STREET
LONDON SW1A 2AA
www.number10.gov.uk

From the Direct Communications Unit   31 January 2013

Dr Laurie Marsh
30 Grove End Road
London
NW8 9LJ

Dear Dr Marsh

I am writing on behalf of the Prime Minister to thank you for the copy of your letter of 20 January addressed to the Secretary of State for Health.

Yours sincerely

Correspondence Officer

Letter from Downing Street acknowledging my
correspondence on RNOH

Despite the lack of a coherent reason for this response, it was obvious our proposal had hit a brick wall. It was hard to make sense of it and my team, who were as bitterly disappointed as me, asked the very obvious question: why?

'The answer is simple,' I told them. 'The civil servants have long championed PFI. It looked great on paper. All the costs were off balance sheet, which the Treasury loved, even though it wasn't *permanently* off the balance sheet and sooner or later the money will have to be paid out.

'There is also an added bonus to PFI: if it all goes wrong they can blame someone else.'

It was a cynical view perhaps, but I didn't think I was far off the mark. It just didn't make sense any other way. My high profile supporters, Basil Feldman and Norman Tebbit, were equally appalled by the turn of events and could make no sense of it either. They lobbied their connections in the House of Lords, but the answer came back that it had been rejected by the civil service, so nothing further could be done.

Time marched on and before long the Prime Minister, who was being kept informed of my offer, carried out a cabinet reshuffle. Andrew Lansley became Lord Privy Seal and Rt Hon Jeremy Hunt took his place as Secretary of State in the Department of Health and Social Security. Although I was technically back to square one, I now had an opportunity to try to get a new Minister on side and convince him how crucial this development could be. It took a couple of months to secure a meeting with Jeremy. Once again I called upon friends in high places to make the necessary introduction. Basil Feldman and Lord Tebbit were both unflinchingly loyal and vocal in my support. When I did finally meet Jeremy Hunt he said he would only be supportive if the local Trust wanted to go ahead with my CFI offer.

'If they don't, I can't help,' he said bluntly. 'There are 20,000 different locations within this great institution we know as the National Health Service. I can't possibly begin arguing with each one, regardless of how good a project looks.'

The arguments rumbled on for more than two more years. In the end, two weeks before the 2010 election, the government, with the Labour party's agreement, went ahead to allow RNOH to embark on what was probably one of the last-ever PFI negotiation options. Unbelievably, the trust opted for a proposal that could well end up costing about £500 million, over one that would mean spending no money at all and would have guaranteed them a healthy cash-flow for the indefinite future. Since that time, Chancellor George Osborne has significantly cooled on PFI and has been vocal about the misuse of them by the Labour Party. It was, however, too late for the RNOH, which in January 2015 abandoned the PFI negotiation and has begun to close down most of its activities at Stanmore. At a time when the NHS is on its knees, it is a bitter pill to swallow.

For a while I was reluctant to get involved with similar projects. Then in May 2014, out of the blue, Southend University Hospital approached me and asked for my help. The hospital is a Foundation Trust on some 33 acres in the centre of Southend, and they explained they were keen on pursuing my CFI idea. I am hopeful that this project will get a chance to succeed where RNOH didn't.

I have become deeply cynical over the years about local authorities and their willingness, or lack thereof, to do anything that falls even slightly out of their comfort zone. In my experience, people who run these organisations on behalf of tax payers are far too wrapped up with themselves, rather than actually working to help the people who pay their wages. One of the most recent instances of this was with Westminster, my own local authority. I approached them with an amazing opportunity that would seriously boost the Council's coffers. I admit, I had a slightly ulterior motive. The Council had announced yet another cut to arts funding and I wanted to save them some money so they might reconsider and help these much needed facilities.

The project I had in mind was based around a rundown set of garages in Maida Vale, which I was told was owned by the Council. I said to the Council, let me use my CFI model to develop this run down mews site. I will draw up plans to convert it into mews houses, employ all the architects, engineers and builders, and make it happen. Once they are finished, I will sell them at the market rate (which would be pretty phenomenal for mews properties in that area) and hand all the money to the Council. It would not cost them one penny, but would bring a return of an estimated £7 million.

You'd have thought they would have bitten my hand off.

They didn't. Indeed, despite first talking about this in 2012, the garages are still lying empty, decaying. After initially saying that it sounded interesting and 'let's explore it', consultants were apparently appointed but have never once met with me face-to-face. I have chased and chased, but the lethargy is astonishing. The development would probably produce a surplus for the taxpayers of Westminster upwards of £8 or £9 million now, but I doubt we'll ever find out.

It is utterly exasperating. I just cannot figure out what is wrong with these political figures who blithely turn their backs on millions of pounds. This is not an isolated example either. As well as the RNOH and this instance in Maida Vale, I also had a run in with Southwark Council. Again, the impetus came from cuts to arts funding, this time to the Unicorn Theatre at London Bridge.

I contacted the Southwark authorities which own at least 20% of the properties in the area and said: 'Give me a list of the derelict ones. I will utilise one or two of them using my CFI model and develop them. Then, I will give you all the money back, every penny. All you need to do is fund the Unicorn Theatre.'

Nothing. They weren't interested. It is just so frustrating. Healthcare and the arts are vital to our communities, but I feel like a lone voice. No one seems to be looking out for tax payers.

Helping others is certainly much easier when you are dealing with private organisations where the parties involved are prepared to listen to ideas, even if they are not immediately familiar. This was certainly the case when I became involved with the Charles Darwin Trust, which was keen to build a new education facility alongside Down House, in Kent, the former home of the English scientist Charles Darwin. Gillian introduced me to Charles Darwin's great grandson Stephen Keynes at a charitable event, and this is where I first heard about his ambitions for the educational facility.

I knew that this charitable development would be tremendously complex. The close association with Darwin ensured that whatever was done would have to be of the highest ecological standards, in line with those that Darwin himself had accepted in his life-time. I had access to copious notebooks of his, which contained details of the plants and trees he had studied, all of which had to be preserved. On the estate itself there were a number of dilapidated buildings dotted around the grounds that had been used for animal research at one time. They were a real eyesore and truly detracted from the historic value of the site. My plan, along with developing the large education centre using my CFI model, included the necessity of replanting a few hundred indigenous trees and shrubs to replace imported ones. This had to be engineered while simultaneously protecting bats, hooded reptiles, slow worms and field mice. Meanwhile, work needed to be carried out to restore the great gardens of a large Arts and Crafts farmhouse known as Buckston Browne to their former glory. My motivation was that a little hard work now would create a lasting legacy for Darwin and his work, and a popular tourist attraction for the county.

After two years of going backwards and forwards, doing my best to appease the local councillors, the Darwin Trust announced they couldn't afford the overheads around the project any longer, even though thus far no one had even managed to put a spade into the ground to start the renovations.

'I'm really sorry,' said Stephen Keynes, when he broke the news. He was clearly distraught that we hadn't been able to see it through.

It was a complex situation. Kirkhouse Trustees, an important national charity, had been responsible for the site's purchase from the Research Group. They had the wholly understandable aim to ensure that animal research ceased on any property linked to the Darwin name. They had also invested about £950,000 to restore Darwin's Home, which has now become a significant tourist attraction run by English Heritage. But now they felt they had to sell this site with its group of derelict old research buildings because of mounting losses.

Stephen Keynes introduced me to the members of the trust and they estimated that they were in line for a loss of about 50%.

'I am prepared, for no cost, to take on the task of a total redesign, appoint a new team of consultants and see if I could, at worst, enable you to receive all of their investment,' I told them. 'Let me just show you what I can achieve.'

Fortunately, this group had enough vision and listened to me. I went ahead and prepared a viability study and, after further consultation, they agreed to allow me to form a trading subsidiary of which I would be sole active director with total authority.

It wasn't plain sailing though. The planning problems were considerable. I had to defer works until the off-season for bat mating! The hooded reptiles, slow worms, and field mice had to be captured by a very expensive specialist, and re-located in similar fields nearby, all of which I had to carefully negotiate. Then the perimeter of the five-acre site needed a deep trench dug around it and an underground fence installed to stop any creatures coming onto the site during the proposed construction. All this when the total recorded number of reptiles and field mice was less than twenty. Perhaps not surprisingly, this section of the preparation took six months at a cost of over £50,000. It didn't end there either as the work required a three year re-checking certification.

The Buckston Browne project was very successful, despite some hiccups

In spite of the delays, the Buckston Browne farmhouse was restored and extended as planned. Four beautiful terraced houses, each with gardens, were created and all sold before they were finished. I had also planned for four large houses on the location previously occupied by the research centre. Unfortunately, a rather intransigent young lady from Bromley Council insisted that the houses were restricted in number so that they would be hidden from the road by the farmhouse in front. I tried to suggest that it could all be solved by moving them a couple of feet to either side, but she wasn't having any of it.

'I am responsible for external design at the planning department and this is my decision,' she announced, getting very cross with me.

I ended up losing a house which would have been worth over £1.5 million – all of which would have been part of the charitable donation to The Kirkhouse Trust. Nevertheless, I completed the project and the other three houses sold easily, taking the total donation to well over two million. Kirkhouse Trust very kindly decided to offer me £150,000 in management fees, all of which I donated to Médecins Sans Frontières.

The key lesson I have learned from my charity work over the past decade or so, is a huge supply of patience is always required. Whether or not it is delays caused by civil service intransigence, or families of field mice that need moving, there is always something standing in the way of progress. However, one can either give up and walk away, or plough on and find a way to make things happen. It's not always possible, as I discovered with RNOH, but hopefully I will go some way to address that disappointment through my work with Southend Hospital. Most of the time it is what it is though. You've just got to grit your teeth and move doggedly forward, despite repeated set-backs. This was certainly my attitude with another of my most recent projects; the Larches Community centre.

In early 2014, at an event in the Waldorf Hotel, to celebrate the joint centenary of the London landmark and the Cinema Exhibitors' Association, I was seated next to Harold Lanning. Harold had been the editor on two of Tigon's most successful films, *Witchfinder General* and *Curse of the Crimson Altar* and I hadn't seen him for many years. As we got reacquainted, I asked him what he was doing now.

'I'm deputy chairman of the British Cinema and Television Veterans and I also chair a charity called Larches Community,' he replied.

I knew the British Cinema and Television Veterans because I was a member, but the Larches I was not familiar with. He explained it was a Jewish charity that aimed to help youngsters and adults with learning difficulties.

'Actually, I am really glad to get some time with you, because I really need some advice,' Harold said. 'I've been watching your career with interest and you are just the person to help us. We desperately need to get more space for Larches. At the moment we are having to turn people away from our community centre. We just can't accommodate them.'

I listened intently as he talked a bit more about the facilities they had. It was obvious this charity was sorely in need of the type of enabling development I'd done elsewhere and one which would guarantee a long-term income.

'I think I could probably help,' I said at last. 'I am afraid I do have a bit of a problem though. I am very secularist in my outlook. I feel uncomfortable with a charity that only looks after people from one religious persuasion. I'm a Jewish Atheist, but I have long come to the conclusion that clans cause all sorts of problems. It would always be my preference to have no clans at all. If you could find a way to open your doors to all disabled people, regardless of religion, then I am more than happy to come on board.'

Harold smiled broadly.

'Leave it with me,' he said.

A short while later a meeting of Larches' Trustees approved the opening up of the charity to a broader range of people, regardless of their religious affiliations and I duly got to work. I managed to find the perfect spot in Edgware and started putting together all the components required to make the development work. As always, I found the local authority rather frustrating to work with. They seemed to take ages to respond to any requests for input or information, and when they did respond, their inclination generally seemed to be to refuse all requests.

This was not the only factor to slow down the development. I had real difficulty in raising funding for the proposal. The sum in question was £3.5 million, which, although it sounds a large sum, is actually quite small in development terms. My usual contacts were simply not interested. Eventually, I secured funds through Big Society Capital, The Charity Bank, which was really very co-operative. They are an independent financial institution dedicated to social investment. Unfortunately, £3.5 million was well beyond their maximum borrowing level, so we had to go back to the drawing board to reduce the cost to £2.5 million.

The local authority and funding delays all took time but I was hopeful we were nearing the end game. Then, just a fortnight before we were due to commit to the project with everything in place, I received a phone call from the vendor of the proposed site.

'I'm afraid we've accepted an offer from an alternative source and they have already paid a £250,000, non-returnable, deposit,' he said. 'I'm very sorry.'

I could barely believe it had happened. We were days away from going ahead and I already had commitment from most of the parties involved. I could have given up and walked away. After all the work I had put in, few would blame me. That's not my style though. While there are still options, I will always explore them, even if they need a bit of lateral thought to get there.

Within a few hours of the fateful call, I was on the phone to Alan Varley and Bruce Robinson, the architects.

We will redevelop The Larches' existing site. Just watch me!

That's just the way things are in business. You can't ever give up.

AFTERWORD

It is natural, when looking back at one's life, to ask yourself: would I have done things differently? Were there things I shouldn't have done? If I had taken this path or that, would things have gone better?

Whenever I begin thinking like this, I often recall one summer in Italy. Gillian and I were married by then. It took us 17 years to tie the knot, but we eventually did in 1995.

This particular year, we had taken our boat away for the summer and Liz had come along too. I still got on well with my ex-wife and she and Gillian became great

Finally! I married Gillian in 1995

friends too. As a family, we loved spending time on our boat, the 45ft yacht 'Marshmellow', and would often go away for weeks at a time, stopping at various ports to meet friends. It felt in some small way like we were continuing a tradition started by my father who loved his boat, and who carried on sailing his 25ft motor yacht, Amanda Jane, right into old age. Indeed, at 80 he spent three months sailing down the coast to Cornwall, living off the fish he caught along the way.

One day, on that particular summer trip down the Amalfi Coast, we moored alongside a charming fishing village and we found a small restaurant for lunch.

We were talking among ourselves when I heard a booming voice.

'Laurie? Laurie Marsh? It is you!'

I swung around in my chair and standing there in front of me was none other than Bond actor Roger Moore. I got up and shook him warmly by the hand and he introduced me to his latest wife, Christina Tholstrup.

'Roger, you've met Gillian haven't you,' I said, smiling as he kissed her on both cheeks. 'And this is Liz, my first wife.'

He looked stunned.

'Your first wife?' he said, slowly. 'You are sitting in a restaurant between your ex-wife and current wife, looking as relaxed and happy as this? How do you do that?'

We all laughed.

'I love them both and they are my pals,' I smiled. 'We often do things together.'

Roger gave a low whistle and then, with a mock

grimace, he said: 'Jesus, it has been costing me millions to pay off my ex-wives, yet all I needed to do was get them together for a plate of Pasta e Fagioli?'

Although things did not work out as well as I had hoped in my marriage to Liz, I always consider it to be one of my greatest achievements that we have remained friends. It has been so important to the harmony of my family and I am so happy that it turned out this way.

My first wife Liz. We married in 1962.

Of course, my other achievement in this respect, are my three wonderful children Mandy (after whom my father named his boat), Robert and Katie, and my three wonderful grand-daughters, Lizey (now in Australia as I write this), Clemmie (at Kings College in Cambridge taking a degree in Classics), and the six-foot baby Frankie, who is still at school. They have, I am proud to say, certainly inherited the hard work gene from me and have all forged great lives for themselves.

While I don't believe in 'luck', because I feel we make our own through endeavour, application and perhaps a little sheer bloody-mindedness, I know I have always been very fortunate throughout my life. The opportunity to go to Perse School, thanks to the hard work and sacrifice of my parents, undoubtedly shaped the rest of my life and contributed to the man I became.

I have also made some fantastic friends along the way, many of whom have been mentioned in this book. Gillian and I have often said the Langford, the Styles, the Rix and the Marshes were the closest little group you could imagine. They have all had a great influence over me and I like to think I have had some positive impact on them too.

Throughout my career I have enjoyed passing on what I have learned to others and am glad that, by spending a little time with people in whom I see great promise, my faith has usually been rewarded.

Perhaps the greatest example of this would be Eric Reynolds. We first met when he was running a number of markets around the country and, as I was running Town Markets at the time, we had a lot in common. I hugely admired his can-do way of doing business, and was not in the least bit surprised when he spearheaded the conversion, refurbishment and management of the now world-famous Camden Lock Market. His forward-thinking created an attraction which brings in more than a quarter-of-a-million visitors a week to the North London borough.

We first worked together in 1992, when we went into partnership to refurbish the Spitalfields Fruit and Vegetable Market and ended up creating the biggest indoor market England has ever seen. The four-and-a-half-acre site was slated for redevelopment at a later stage, but Eric created a proposal to keep it going while the plans were being developed. While I helped him with the documentation to fight off the developers, he created a market for people of all ages, with attractions such as an Organic Market and an Alternative Fashion Market. He even installed an Olympic-sized pool and a model train that ran around the perimeter. Artists were employed to redecorate the run-down, graffiti-strewn area with pictures of flowers and fruits. Eventually more than 2,000 people were employed there. Not surprisingly, the locals loved it, even though it was under constant threat of closure by planners eager to build an office block there. Eric's grand finale, which I fully supported, was to build an opera house on site. It was tragic when the lease finally expired in 1999 and it all had to be pulled down, but we'd made a profit, had a great time in doing it, and provided a fantastic focal point for the community.

Eric's next venture was to try and stop The City selling Smithfield Market to a property company who intended to keep some facades but build a range of high rise, modern office buildings inside the site. This would have destroyed the interior and created the loss of this valuable and historic monument for ever. Eric needed to prove viability in injunction legal proceedings and he asked me to help in that connection. I delivered a letter of financial support for presentation to the Court on 21st February 2014. Eric was successful, Smithfield Market has been saved. It was a pleasure and a privilege to work with him and to bounce ideas off each other.

Eric created another business called 'Container City'. He tendered to build the Media Centre at the London Olympics and his offer was well below the minimum tender price. It was the same old story; 'It is too good to be true so ...' He went on to save several million of lottery fund pounds and in 2015 rebuilt the containers into an office block at his base on Trinity Buoy Wharf. He's also built another similar container complex adjoining the Roundhouse.

As well as being very fortunate to have known my close circle of friends, albeit too briefly in some cases, my life has been marked by many happy coincidences too, perhaps nowhere more so than in my hobby of collecting art. I have always been a passionate lover of art and have amassed an impressive collection over the years.

Take my experience with Lola as a case in point. I came across the Italian-born sculptor Enzo Plazzotta via my connection with the dancers Antoinette Sibley and Anthony Dowell at the Royal Opera House. Enzo was sculpting the pair and I bought a sculpture of each of them and one Romeo and Juliet version of the pair together. Through my patronage, I got to know Enzo and we got on well. I began to visit him often at his studio in Chelsea and on one of these occasions I spotted an extraordinary sculpture of a woman. She was not yet quite finished, but Enzo told me she was called Lola and I knew then and there Lola must be mine. She was, quite simply, exquisite. We negotiated a price and agreed on the sale.

A short while later Enzo died. He had been ill with cancer for a while, but no one realised how poorly he was. I went to the funeral and paid my respects, but didn't mention Lola to his stepson or his wife. It wasn't the right time. After a respectful gap, I got in contact with Enzo's stepson to remind him of my agreement.

'Oh, no, we've sold Lola,' he said matter-of-factly.

I was stunned. I could hardly believe that this was the end of Lola.

Twenty years later, I was with Gillian, driving down one of the lovely side streets in St James, looking for somewhere to park, when I glanced at a shop window. There, looking more beautiful than ever, was Lola. It must have been fate. The dealer had a telephone number on the gallery front. I called at 9am prompt the following morning. It turned out that Lola's price tag had gone up by 400% in the intervening two decades, but I negotiated hard. I told the shop owner about my previous connection with Lola and my agreement with Enzo, and eventually managed to get the sculpture down to a price I was prepared to pay. I often say that Lola evaded me for twenty years, but now she is back where she belongs. She sits in pride of place in the courtyard, just outside my office window, and every time I catch sight of her I smile.

Lola was not the only instance of my good fortune in collecting. In the mid-eighties, I was rather pleased to have acquired a number of pieces by the talented forger Elmyr de Hory. The Hungarian-born painter's work was so flawless that many experts were completely fooled. Indeed, the family of Raoul Dufy were known to have rejected Dufy's own paintings in favour of authenticating de Hory's! I thought it would be a fascinating to own some of his work, so when I spotted an ad in the Financial Times offering a number of his paintings, I snapped them up. Once I bought them, I gave one to Liz and bequeathed the rest to my children. Years later, I had a particular portrait examined in detail by Sir Roy Strong. I could barely believe it when this picture, *Lady with Rose* 'by' Auguste Renoir, with the Louvre of Paris sign on its back, was judged to be authentic. Instead of a fake worth a respectable £10,000, I had apparently been sold a genuine Renoir which was worth much, much more. In reality though, it is worth nothing more than I paid for it. It is not for sale and it belongs to the children.

Another characteristic of my life is things often seem to come full circle. I never seem to get very far away from Mayfair, one way or another, and in particular Park Street. My first association with the place was right at the beginning of my career. 106 Park Street was head office of Blacketts Department Store group and its charismatic yet flawed boss, Claude Kingsley Rudkin-Jones. I was only employed by Blacketts for about eighteen months before that all blew up and I moved on to other things. Later, my daughter Mandy's partner Steve Bowring, father to my three grandchildren, was employed by The Carlisle Group at 104 Park Street. Then, a couple of years later, I received a cry for help from a young man who'd been working at my house for some time installing my surround sound cinemas as well as equipment for my Hi-Fi. Sosthy, as we knew him, told me his friend from university, Morgan Brown, who was now Head of Chancery at the Ghanaian High Commission, had got himself into a terrible pickle. He was a high flyer and due to be awarded a higher grade post somewhere in Europe, but this was now in jeopardy

Morgan Brown was responsible for the Ghana Estate Properties in UK and had granted a 21-year lease of the Trade Commission to a third party after the High Commission had relocated to a larger building elsewhere. These tenants had wrecked the place.

'They've stolen everything,' Sosthy said, looking shocked and crestfallen. 'When this gets found out, Morgan could be sent back to Ghana in disgrace. No one will ever hear from him again, I am sure of that. You have had many years of experience with property. Would you be able to take a look at the building and see what can be done?'

'Of course,' I said, straight away. I liked Sosthy, who had been improving the sound of music in my life. Where is the Ghana Trade Centre building exactly?'

'102 Park Street, Mayfair.'

I couldn't help but smile to myself, I knew that location well.

Sosthy probably didn't realise the extent of the problem that was facing his friend Morgan and the High

Commission. The Duke of Westminster, the effective owner of Grosvenor Estates, insisted upon the very highest possible standards of quality for estate buildings and even nominated and sourced specially selected materials for repairs or rebuilding which were invariably very expensive indeed.

The Head of Chancery was so keen to find out if I could save the building for them that he sent a chauffeur driven limo to take me there for a thorough survey. When I toured the Trade Commission I quickly discovered these friends had not just stolen a few fixtures and fittings. The fine interior of the imposing, brick-built, six storey building was totally wrecked. They'd made off with the carpets, furniture, telephones, artwork, desks, everything. They'd also caused substantial structural damage: the roof was open to the skies and the basement was flooded. I arranged for a survey by Michael Collins Associates for the records.

The state in which we had found this very important building was very serious indeed, not least because the Ghanaian High Commission had paid the best part of £1 million for their 99-year lease, and it still had 92 years left to run. The Grosvenor Estate, which owned the building, got wind of what was happening and immediately served notice that they would request a forfeiture of the lease and take back possession of the building if the Ghanaians didn't correct the damage, the cost of which was unknown to The High Commission.

I decided to accept this challenge and immediately stepped in, beginning by negotiating a stay-of execution from Grosvenor Estates who fortunately knew me. To secure funding, I required the granting of a sub-underlease for the full term of the head-lease to a new company which I formed, called '102 Park Street Developments Ltd'. I also had to obtain the approval of The Grosvenor Estate for these legal arrangements. I then had to obtain consent to my proposed schedule of works, not only from the Local Authority in Westminster, since external roof-works were involved, but also from Grosvenor Estates, which was much more difficult.

The logistics of the project were far more complex than usual, not least because the Ghanainans were not at all well advised. I had to hold their hands through every step, and even helped appoint a lawyer to act for them on the transaction because they didn't have one with commercial property knowledge. I was in the slightly ludicrous situation of finding a legal expert to act against myself. That was certainly another first for me.

I arranged for an updated valuation of the property based upon a large number of improvements for which I now had consent, which in turn had added to the value. The market had also moved up in the meantime, which was fortunate. I employed specialist contractors and renovated the whole place, adding some additional useable large spaces by converting the rear stable and yard sheds into well-lit open offices and building in a modern, fully-fitted kitchen in the basement. I also put in a lift, air conditioning and rebuilt the roof.

Once I had control of the situation, a replacement Head of Chancery, Sena Siaw-Boateng, was appointed and quickly appraised of the background. She and I spent quite a lot of time together and there was a period of about nine months when I was asked to look into all Chancery matters for the High Commission. The scope of my remit expanded exponentially. I was asked to advise and help on all sorts of matters and for a while I was forever in and out of The High Commission at 13 Belgrave Square. In effect, I took on the role as a sort of 'Associate Head of Chancery'. I didn't mind at all. In fact, I found it all rather stimulating.

The project was a complete success. I raised all the finance for the scheme, spending the best part of £2 million on the works, which were exquisitely designed by Michael Collins. When I had finished, I sold my lease to the new tenants called Endless Corporation, which had to be approved by both the Grosvenor Estate and the High Commission. They now pay a very respectable rent to the High Commission. My intervention also saved the Ghanaians from paying the £2 million for the extensions and reinstatement, as well as a further million which they would have lost if their lease had been forfeited. A loss of this size would have been tremendously damaging to the High Commission.

I earned a decent fee from the purchasers and some heartfelt thanks from the High Commissioner, His Excellency Annan Arkiyan Kato, who introduced me to President John Atta Mills at their next official function. I was told my efforts to save the treasury from substantial losses were very much appreciated and invited to visit Ghana as a guest. The Ghanaian High Commission still invites me to parties even today and the most recent High Commissioner Professor Kwaku Danso-Boafo has been just as welcoming.

Having noted down all my stories it may seem as though the various chapters in my life are now closed. In fact, this is far from the truth and I still have a number of projects in the pipeline. The Larches scheme is on-going, and then there is something that has occupied much of my time over the past seven years and will no doubt do so for the next seven: the putative Cinema Museum in my birth borough of Lambeth. The Museum currently on the site is housed in an NHS-owned building which was constructed as a workhouse about 170 years ago. The curators and founders, Ronald Grant and Martin Humphries, have been collecting cinema related artefacts for about 50 years and have a wonderfully eccentric collection of movie memorabilia. It is my dream, and that of many high profile supporters from stage and screen, to turn it into one of London's premier tourist attractions. It is utterly the right place for it too. This was the workhouse where Charlie Chaplin and his brother Syd lived with his mother during his very early years. I couldn't think of anywhere more apt to have a museum charting the history of the Big Screen, from the early days of silent movies to the modern blockbusters we see today.

Of course, as with all major projects, nothing is ever straight forward. The local authorities are not the biggest bugbear this time: in this scheme that accolade goes to the NHS. A subsidiary of the health body known by the apt acronym SLaM owns the site and no sooner do we persuade one executive to grant a lease and negotiate terms for us to buy the freehold, then there is a change of personnel and we have to start the whole process over again. At the time of writing, the negotiations have been going on for over seven years. A new CEO was appointed around October 2014, but he was no longer there by March 2015. This is a great disappointment to me and the team since he was a really enthusiastic supporter of our intentions. He even brought his children for a tour and made a personal donation to the Museum.

Another big stumbling block has been a former care home on the site which has been empty for many years. SLaM agreed to have it valued over two years ago, but the fellow from Savills they sent round only stayed half-an-hour and never came back with a valuation. After a few more changes of personnel, they repeated the exercise recently – right down to the chap from Savills coming round for a brief visit and then not coming back with a valuation. In the end, I paid to have a valuation by Gerald Eve LLP who have carried out a Red Book projected valuation of £15,130,000, subject to an appropriate planning consent. In its present state, the whole site is worth around £4 million. SLaM property department have indicated a similar projected valuation, subject to planning, so we are finally getting somewhere.

I have recently introduced Family Mosaic, the large housing association who had an historic and direct relationship with the site, since they took over the affordable housing within the Bellway housing project on the same estate in 2010. They have an enormous portfolio valued at about £1,250,000,000 of housing assets and they have now agreed to fund the whole project for us.

I'm confident we will get there in the end. I am very much looking forward to the time I can see the portrait of Charlie Chaplin, created by acclaimed artist Sean Alexander, in the foyer of the museum. It currently hangs in my office and every time I look at it I am determined to see this scheme to fruition.

My latest project takes me back to my entertainment roots: The Mill Theatre at Sonning Eye. It is a truly extraordinary venue on a tiny island where the Thames splits at Sonning Eye in Oxfordshire. A mill was established there, which produced flour for Huntley and Palmer biscuits in the 19th and early 20th centuries and has been, more recently, converted into a 215-seat theatre, with a restaurant.

My old friend Ray Cooney brought Sonning to my attention, during the run of one of his plays over the Christmas period of 2014. The present owner, actress Sally Hughes, was attempting to raise money. She and her advisors had decided to do so by selling shares, and they had prepared a complicated loan agreement for investors in the facility which they were targeting at theatre lovers. Ray forwarded one to me.

'What do you think about this?' he asked in the accompanying note. 'Looks like one for you.'

He was right. I immediately made arrangements to meet Sally and she was very eager to show me around the theatre and the various building attached to the complex. As she showed me around, she explained that she desperately needed money for repairs.

'Someone is going to fall into one of the potholes in the car park,' she half-joked.

'I'm not sure selling shares is a very good idea,' I said. 'You will create an inordinate amount of paperwork to raise £500 here or £1000 there, and then you'll have to keep in constant touch with your shareholders to update them on their investment. You'd be better off using your talent and energies on your productions.'

I did not have to tell her that her family's ownership of this amazing island on the Thames at Sonning was a very valuable asset and was, indeed, far more so now. Hollywood 'A' lister George Clooney and his new wife Amal had just bought Mill House, which adjoined the theatre, so the entire island was very hot property indeed.

'You could use some of the extensive existing buildings more effectively and part of the car park land might be suitable for a couple of houses, but this will not be easy,' I said. 'The Mill is a listed building and this inhibits any construction work and, of course, it is located in a conservation area subject to flooding.'

'If your ideas go ahead, how much will that cost?' she said doubtfully.

'Nothing,' I said, smiling as her eyes widened in shock. 'If I can obtain a satisfactory planning consent, I can arrange funding for the whole project using the freehold with consent as security. For planning purposes the project is called an enabling development.'

Comprehensive structural and site surveys have been

carried out together with flood risk assessments and environmental studies. All of the preparatory work is now completed and draft plans prepared. These have now been discussed in a pre-planning application with the local planning and conservation authorities who have been supportive. If and when it all goes ahead, money will be spent on renovating and technically upgrading the theatre and on refurbishing the restaurant to make it a top quality venue. The setting is already marvellous. With a gourmet menu and upmarket fixtures, an eatery in this position could be a gold mine. I have prepared a five-point 'wish list' that is ambitious but entirely achievable.

My target is to create a long-term income for The Mill Theatre at Sonning Eye in order to support future productions. I know from experience that a theatre that size could never make profit from ticket sales alone. My proposals are designed to create a sufficiently large capital sum to pay off accumulated debt and also to provide funding for bringing the whole theatre interior and exterior up to 21st century standards. If all goes to plan, the venue will continue to be the most important arts facility in this highly desirable area of England. As I write, I have a sense of how successful this project might be. The Mill's esteemed neighbour George Clooney is already helping out. He is having his Listed home restored, and his manager has already agreed to pay for resurfacing the shared road. All of the research has been completed, and the principal consultants have all contributed their valuable services on a speculative basis. It's all systems go!

In December, I was asked if I would advise the

executives of Wilts and Berks Canal Trust and the Swindon Redevelopment Team about a vast new project that had been waiting for guidance and inspiration for some years. I agreed to do so and I believe that under my guidance a new 70 mile long canal is now part of one of the largest projects in Europe and is finally 'moving forwards'. The approximate cost estimate is well over £1 billion.

I'm sure that this won't be the last of my philanthropic or commercial projects. I'm still coming up with ideas all the time and am constantly being approached for advice. I feel as strongly about getting on with things today as when I was a young army recruit, just itching to get out into the world and make something of myself. I guess I am just not the retiring type.

The one question I will always be asking myself is: what's next?

Laurie Marsh is a philanthropic entrepreneur with a very wide range of commercial and charitable experience developed over 65 years of business ventures. Born in 1930, he lived for 8 years in a couple of rooms above a family haberdasher in Lambeth Walk. After army conscription, Laurie then started a plastics manufacturing business and obtained consent to licence Walt Disney cartoon characters. He also became a director of a family property company, set up a partnership with West End Travel Group, and carried out his first £1 million building project in central Derby in 1961 (eventually creating the third largest public property company in the UK).

Laurie has developed and operated hotels, theatres in London and New York, a 150 screen cinema chain, produced over 75 films and founded an international distribution company. When he sold the conglomerate business in 1979 he then embarked on multi-million pound philanthropic ventures which are ongoing to this day.